MAY ONE BELIEVE—
IN RUSSIA?

MAY ONE BELIEVE— IN RUSSIA?

Violations of Religious Liberty in the Soviet Union

Edited by Michael Bourdeaux
and Michael Rowe in collaboration
with the International Committee
for the Defence of Human Rights
in the USSR, Brussels

KESTON BOOK NO. 19

Darton, Longman & Todd
London

First published in 1980
Darton, Longman & Todd Ltd
89 Lillie Road
London SW6 1UD

© 1980 Keston College

ISBN 0 232 51507 7

Printed in Great Britain by
The Anchor Press Ltd
and bound by Wm. Brendon and Son Ltd
both of Tiptree, Essex

CONTENTS

Editors' Preface

This volume first appeared in 1975 under the title *White Book on Restrictions of Religion in the USSR* and was published privately by Major-General Albert Guérisse (Ret'd), President of the International Committee for the Defence of Human Rights in the USSR, 100 avenue Général Lartigue, B-1200 Brussels, Belgium. We gratefully acknowledge the research grant from the International Committee that enabled the original version to be compiled and the subsequent grant from the Committee for the updating and expansion of the book for a second edition.

The guarantee of human rights, including religious freedom—the right to believe—was an integral part of the Helsinki Agreements of 1975, which called in the preamble for freedom for all citizens to worship 'in accordance with the dictates of their own conscience'. The right to believe, 'to profess any religion or none', in the words of the Soviet Constitution, implies the right to act in accordance with one's beliefs. It is this right which is severely restricted by Soviet law and administrative practice.

Foreword

In the course of the twelve years of its existence, the centre for studying religion in Communist Lands (Keston College) has acquired a reputation for meticulous accuracy, as well as for scholarly objectivity in the sense that it never allows its avowed sympathy with those who adhere to religious beliefs and practices to affect its respect for facts. I very much hope that this book will reach a wide public.

The importance of the theme with which it deals—the restrictions to which believers of all faiths and denominations are subjected in the USSR—can hardly be exaggerated. To believers outside the USSR, of course, this importance is obvious. But even for those who feel themselves to be agnostic, reliable information on the way in which the Soviet authorities treat the various religious communities in their country is of vital significance as a test of the persistent Soviet claim that religious tolerance is strictly observed in the USSR, that no one is ever persecuted for his beliefs or opinions, and that in all cases where believers have been sentenced by the courts or administratively punished this has been for their criminal activities, and not for their beliefs. The documents reprinted in this collection will enable the reader to judge for himself how far this Soviet claim is true. This is particularly important in a year when Soviet observance of the Final Act of the Helsinki agreement once again comes up for review.

This collection of notes and documents also offers striking evidence of the growing strength of religious observance and unshakeable faith in a country in which atheist propaganda has been vigorously pursued by the government for decades; and where the practice, let alone propagation, of religion is fraught with grave risks.

Let no one fear that a scholarly collection of this kind will contribute to what is called the 'cold war'. Years of experience have proved beyond argument that the real hope of improvement of relations with the Soviet Union does not lie in hypocrisy and concealment, in sweeping under the carpet the things which ought to be criticized. Such conduct on our part may have given the illusion of good relations for a year or two, but has always ended in greater hostility when the truth could no longer be concealed. The only hope for better relations with the Soviet Union lies in open and frank discussion of those aspects of Soviet policy which we find repugnant. There is only one condition to be observed— and that is that we get our facts right. This collection is designed as an aid to that end.

Let us never forget that we owe our knowledge of the plight of religion in the USSR to the supreme courage of those who risk their liberty, their health and their livelihood to inform those of us who live in a free country of what goes on in a society where totalitarian rule prevails. These heroes and martyrs are in the forefront of the struggle for a spiritual revival in the USSR. If freedom should ever come to be in that unhappy country, it will in no small measure be due to the efforts of those who strive, in the face of great odds, to keep alive the word of God and spiritual values.

LEONARD SCHAPIRO

London School of Economics and Political Science,
May, 1980

Introduction

DOCUMENT 1:
AN APPEAL TO CHRISTIANS THROUGHOUT THE WORLD

'But the Lord shall endure for ever:
he hath prepared his throne for
judgement.' (Ps. 9:7)

*From prisoners of various faiths in the Sosnovka concentration camp,
Mordovia.*

Can faith be destroyed? In the pagan world, Christians were persecuted, killed, thrown into dungeons and handed over to be torn
to pieces by wild animals. Cruelty and violence, however, failed
to overcome those who had been converted to Christ, and it was
they who conquered. The Spirit and Faith triumphed over the
sword, the dungeon and the mightiest pagan power of the ancient
world. Two thousand years have passed, and the words of Christ
have spread throughout the world and transformed it. That world
has become more humane, more civilized, tolerant towards those
who hold different opinions. It has proclaimed freedom of conscience to be the corner-stone of modern civilization. The world
has become so tolerant that it allowed the setting up of an atheist
state and not only accepted its existence, but also moved towards
peaceful co-existence and co-operation in the best interests of mankind. Is it possible to mistrust a state that has signed the Declaration
of Human Rights and the Helsinki Agreement, that has ratified the
International Convention on Civil and Political Rights and that
proclaims in its constitution freedom of conscience and religious
belief to be an inalienable right of its citizens?

Has the Christian world made a mistake in trusting an atheist
state? Has the time come for a reconciliation between the Christian
world and Satan, glorying in his defiance of God? Has Satan
renounced his aims and ceased to be an enemy of God and those
who believe in him? Has he abandoned the persecution of Christ-

ians? Of course, Christians are not publicly thrown to the lions in the Soviet Union today. It prefers less obvious methods of dealing with them. Nor are Christians used as human torches along the sides of the roads, and it would seem that this is not just because these roads are used by tourists from Western countries.

The two thousand years that have passed since the persecutions of pagan Rome have inevitably had their effect upon the methods used to deal with Christians. In the Soviet Union they are not burned alive or thrown to the lions, they are 'simply' subjected to a limitation of their rights and the obstinate are sent to concentration camps. However, Satan is not so easily satisfied, and even here in the camp continues to persecute and mock the believers. Here is a recent example.

17 June, the 'Sosnovka' camp. The camp commandant summoned one of the prisoners to his office and ordered him to remove the cross he was wearing. The prisoner refused to obey such an arbitrary command, pointing out that the Constitution proclaims freedom of conscience and freedom of belief and religious worship. The correctional-labour code specifically omits to limit these rights with regard to prisoners. He declared that the cross was the symbol of the Christian faith, that it was sacred, and that its forcible removal was an offence against the feelings of a believer. He also attempted to appeal to common humanity, but the commandant had already sent for a warder and ordered him to remove the cross from the prisoner. Thus began the removal of all crosses worn by prisoners in the Sosnovka correctional labour camp, which is used for political detainees. Those subjected to this treatment, as well as a few other prisoners, went on a hunger-strike to protest at this outrage against their faith. After such an act, how can the declaration in the Soviet Constitution on freedom of conscience and religious belief appear as anything but a lie? How can the statements by the Soviet Union, assuring the world that it is concerned with upholding human rights, appear as anything but hypocrisy? Has it not rather used the Declaration on Human Rights and the Helsinki Agreement as a fig-leaf to hide its violation of basic freedoms within its own borders?

If the Soviet Union respected the fundamental right to freedom of conscience and religious worship, prisoners would not only be able to wear a cross but would also be able to possess a Bible, prayer books and icons. At present, Christians in prison are deprived of the basic items of their faith. One is reminded of the chapter 'The smile of the buddha' from *The First Circle* by Solzhenitsyn. In order to impress the wife of President Roosevelt, who expressed the wish to visit a Soviet prison during her visit to the USSR, the Butyrki administration brought to the cell of the starving prisoners not only a pan of porridge but also a Bible and a statue of Buddha which were placed on a red linen cloth covering the locker. The administration wanted to show not only that Soviet prisoners were well fed, but also that they enjoyed freedom of conscience and religious worship. As soon as Eleanor Roosevelt left the prison-cell these signs of the religious rights of the prisoners disappeared. Throughout the entire history of Soviet power they appeared in one prison for one day and then disappeared for ever. Will the day ever dawn when believers in Soviet prisons will be able to possess a Bible and prayer books, crosses, a statue of Buddha, the Koran or other articles relating to their faith and testifying to the reality of freedom of conscience and of religious worship?

Two thousand years ago, Christians underwent savage persecution and emerged triumphant. Is it not time for those who organized the 'hounding' of Christians in the Sosnovka concentration camp and for all those on whom depends the implementation of the rights of believers in the USSR to ponder over the glorious two-thousand-year history of the Christian faith? Is it not time to carry the Bible into the cells and barracks and leave them there for ever? Is it not time to declare a general amnesty for all political prisoners and to end the persecution of Christians and all those who hold different opinions? This would prove that the signatures on the Declaration of Human Rights and the Helsinki Agreement are not just a pharasaical and hypocritical exercise in political manœuvring.

We, the undersigned, political prisoners in the Sosnovka concentration camp, declare that everything written here is the truth, and we appeal to all Christians throughout the world to defend our right to worship and to protect our religious feelings from offence and outrage. Demand freedom for political prisoners in the Soviet Union.

3 July 1979.

B. Gajauskas, N. Yevgrafov, S. Karavansky, L. Lukyanenko, A. Murzhenko, B. Rebrik, I. Stepanov, Yu. Fedorov, D. Shumuk.

I.

The Law[1]

It has sometimes been said that, if only the authorities would abide by their own laws, the major areas of discrimination in the Soviet Union would disappear. Such statements are, at best, only partly true, for although there are certain guarantees of the individual's rights contained in the Constitution (technically the 'supreme law'), the fact is that the Penal Code can, in practice, negate what are supposed to be the superior freedoms of the Constitution. In no area is this contradiction more damaging to the rights of the individual than that of religious life.

The Soviet law, as at present formulated, declares church and state to be separated. It further makes it quite clear that discrimination against the individual for reasons of his religious adherence is a punishable offence. These, originally, were Leninist principles. The first-ever decree of the Soviet state on religion, in the formulation of which Lenin himself had a considerable say, proclaimed that it was illegal 'to restrain or limit freedom of conscience' and that 'every citizen may profess any religion or none at all'. This was logically reflected in the first Constitution (July 1918), which stated that 'the right to religious and anti-religious propaganda is recognized for all citizens'.

The right to 'religious propaganda' was obviously a highly significant principle—indeed, to Stalin it was an emotive one, which was not compatible with his policy of gathering every strand of Soviet public life under his personal scrutiny or the direct control of the secret police. The basic legislation, 'On Religious Associations', was promulgated on 8 April 1929 and it reflects, in almost every one of its 68 paragraphs, the determination of an emergent dictatorship to impose itself totally upon religious life throughout the land. This law would obviously have made a mockery of the Constitution if the latter had been left unchanged. Therefore, the Constitution was modified a month later (18 May 1929) to exclude the right to 'religious propaganda'; the right of

---

[1] A more detailed version of this chapter may be found in *Religious Minorities in the Soviet Union*, prepared by CSRC (Centre for the Study of Religion and Communism) for Minority Rights Group, London, 3rd edn 1977.

'religious profession' was substituted (contrasted with the right of anti-religious propaganda). Significantly, the Stalinist law, 'On Religious Associations', stands to the present day, with only minor amendments.

Even more significant are the provisions of penal (as opposed to civil) legislation. Under Stalin many believers were sentenced to 10–25 year terms of imprisonment under the notorious article 58 of the Criminal Code on charges of anti-Soviet agitation or belonging to an anti-Soviet organization. In the process of de-Stalinization the Criminal Code was revised and the RSFSR Code of 1959 contained two articles, 142 and 227, which relate exclusively to religious activity. Although the penalties, three and five years respectively, are milder than those imposed under article 58, they virtually guarantee the conviction of any person engaged in the leadership of religious groups not recognized by the secular authorities. The wording of both articles is deliberately vague, though an official clarification of article 142 was issued in 1966, which heralded its wide-scale application to *Initsiativniki* Baptists.

Even supposing it were possible completely to clarify the published legislation, this would still not shed sufficient light upon current Soviet practice towards religion. This is because we know for a fact that some areas of religious life are regulated by secret laws. To quote the most obvious example, the Council on Religious Affairs, the government's central controlling body, has no proper basis in any published source. This body is known to pass on to its local representatives whole series of secret instructions which sometimes go well beyond the public laws. Some of these instructions are included in a volume published in 1971 and intended for official use only, a copy of which reached the West.[2] However, it is not considered necessary for the believers affected by these instructions to be informed of either their existence or their precise contents. Inevitably, therefore, if we approach Soviet practice towards religion from a purely legal standpoint, we find ourselves faced with many contradictions. It is all part of the pattern that the penalties for discriminating against believers on the grounds of their religion appear never—or at best very rarely— to have been invoked, though there has been occasional restitution of rights to believers who have been illegally deprived. At the same time every clause of the law which could restrict the basic

---

[2] See *Religion in Communist Lands* vol. iv, no. 4, Winter 1976, pp. 24–31, Walter Sawatsky, 'Secret Soviet Lawbook on Religion'.

human rights of Soviet believers has been exploited in the last twenty years, not to mention a number of practices which have no basis in public legality. The basic lot of the average Soviet believer seems to have been less severe under Brezhnev and Kosygin than under Khrushchev in his later years—yet the existing framework of past practice and present legislation offers no future security against a new physical anti-religious campaign such as took place in 1960–64, and, indeed, there are signs that the situation is again worsening.

Here are some signposts (not an exhaustive list) to the types of discrimination which have been practised towards religious believers in the Soviet Union within the last decade or more. Not all categories apply equally to all religious denominations.

(i) *Outlawing of a whole denomination.* There is no published legal basis for this and it must be regulated by a secret decree. (Eastern-Rite Catholics in 1946, Pentecostals, Jehovah's Witnesses, many sectarian offshoots of the Orthodox Church and the Old Believers, etc.)

(ii) *Enforced merging with other denominations, losing individual traditions.* There is no legal basis for this. (Uniates from 1948 could continue to worship only by becoming Orthodox; the Pentecostals could become accepted from 1945 by merging with Baptists; similarly Evangelical Christians from 1944 and Mennonites from 1963)

(iii) *Enforced closure of legally-existing places of worship.* After the passing of the 1929 law, very few congregations could in fact register, but many did during and after World War II. In 1960–64 there was a massive illegal closure of places of worship throughout the Soviet Union. Only a very few of those closed churches have since been re-opened.

(iv) *State control of all legally-existing places of worship.* This is achieved by the registration regulations enforced by the supplying of lists of members to communist authorities and the right of veto by those authorities over the membership of the executive body. These provisions at the same time break the fundamental constitutional requirement of the separation of church and state. There are many documented instances of refusal by the authorities to grant registration. The authorities are not legally obliged to state reasons for refusing registration, but must say yes or no within a month of receiving the application. Often they simply do not reply. There is known also to be illegal state interference in church appointments. A secret instruction provides for the registration of clergy.

(v) *Banning of all religious activities, except worship within registered churches.* For worship anywhere else, permission must be sought two weeks in advance for each individual instance; it is often not granted. The clergy's activity is restricted to their own areas. There is an absolute ban on all relief work. No parish societies or discussion groups may be organized. The law technically does not ban the production of religious literature, provided it does not call for 'infringement of the law'—but *de facto* it is treated as illegal except for the single central periodical and occasional inadequate editions of calendars, the Bible, prayer and hymn books produced by some denominations. All Sunday schools are banned—as is informal religious instruction for minors; restrictions are placed even on that given by parents to their own children. Permission must be sought for any 'special theological courses' for the training of clergy. The existence of permanent theological seminaries is not recognized in law and presumably their existence would end at once if the 'special permission' were to be withdrawn. No other religious institutions whatever are recognized in law, though the Orthodox and Armenian Churches retain a few monasteries. Many existing monasteries were closed in the early 1960s.

(vi) *No religious association (parish) is a person at law.* Therefore, no parish can contest its rights at law, nor can it formally apply for redress.

(vii) *No central representative bodies.* No provision for these is recognized by the law. Discrimination is exercised here: Orthodox, Old Believers, Baptists, Moslems and Buddhists are allowed representative bodies; Jews, Roman Catholics are denied them. That of the Adventists was abolished in 1960. This is a violation of the principle of separation of church and state.

(viii) *Restrictions on local and national congresses.* These may be held with especial permission—but *de facto* take place only in the rarest instances. Baptists alone have, since 1963, established the principle of regular congresses; they met in 1963, 1966, 1969, 1974 and 1979. (All the above restrictions are in some sense related to the law; those which follow have no basis whatever in law—indeed, the 1966 elaboration of art. 142 of the Penal Code theoretically protects religious believers from them.)

(ix) *Defamation in the press without right to reply.* This has been frequently practised against all denominations.

(x) *Rooting out of old religious customs.* There has been an attempt to replace them by 'new socialist traditions'.

(xi) *Discrimination at places of work.* This is strictly illegal, though still practised.

(xii) *Discrimination in housing.* There has sometimes been a refusal (strictly illegal) to grant adequate housing for religious believers; houses used—sometimes with permission—for religious gatherings have been attacked, with windows smashed and doors broken down.

(xiii) *Discrimination in education.* Quite apart from the restrictions on religious education noted in item (v) above, believers are often quite illegally denied equal opportunities in secular education. Religious children at school often have to bear scorn from teachers and other pupils. Students are often expelled from colleges and universities if their faith is discovered.

(xiv) *Discrimination in public life.* Known believers of all types are with very few exceptions effectively prevented from reaching positions of authority and are, therefore, being discriminated against 'publicly', as it were. There are some known instances where believers have, for example, been expelled from the Communist Party, from managerial positions or from teaching posts. It is a nationwide feature of Soviet life, however, that believers are almost always prevented from reaching such positions in the first place— even from entering higher education. This phenomenon is difficult to document, though it is made explicit in Party pronouncements on religion and is well known to all observers of the Soviet scene. It is mainly in the world of the arts that there are persons known to be believers active in public life, though individual instances have been reported in the scientific sphere and even the higher military command. Such political and social discrimination at a very early stage in the person's life inevitably leads to an economic discrimination also—the emergence of believers as a huge group of second-class citizens (in an economic as well as civil rights sense) throughout the Soviet Union.

Over the last decade, there have been thousands of documented instances of the use of the full force of the law against believers, not to mention the existence of cases which we do not know about, in numbers which may only be guessed. Crippling fines have been widely imposed, often repeatedly on the same people, for organizing religious worship (the one 'constitutional right' of every Soviet believer)—often in cases where registration has been applied for, but not granted.

Orthodox and Uniate believers (from bishops down), Jehovah's Witnesses, Roman Catholics, Baptists, Adventists and Pentecostals have been imprisoned for three or five years, sometimes even longer, for activities which are not considered criminal by the great majority of other countries in the world. Even some other communist countries permit religious practices which are considered illegal in the USSR (for example religious instruction for children). In many documentable instances, false accusations of moral delinquency have been brought.

Special punishments have been meted out to those who have attempted to continue their religious observances in prison. There are a few known instances of where the especially harsh conditions to which believers have often been subjected in prison or during interrogation have led to serious injury or even to death under torture.

DOCUMENT 2:
EXTRACT FROM 'LAW ON RELIGIOUS ASSOCIATIONS' ARTICLE 17

'Religious associations are forbidden:
(a) to create mutual aid funds, cooperatives, producer associations and in any way to use the property at their disposal for any purposes other than the satisfaction of religious needs;
(b) to give material support to their members;
(c) to organize special meetings for children, young people, or prayer meetings or other meetings for women, or general meetings, groups, circles or sections for Bible study, study of literature, handicrafts or work, or to organize excursions and children's playgrounds, to open libraries or reading rooms, to set up sanatoria or medical aid programmes.

In prayer buildings and premises only those books may be stored which are necessary for the conduct of the cult in question.'

DOCUMENT 3:
EXTRACTS FROM OFFICIAL COMMENTARY ON THE LAW ON RELIGIOUS ASSOCIATIONS

The Ukrainian atheist monthly Lyudyna i svit (Man and the World) *in its June 1978 issue (pp. 16–20) published a commentary on the revised*

'Regulations on religious associations in the Ukrainian SSR'. This commentary written by O. Havrylyuk, is entitled 'Legal Guarantees of Freedom of Conscience'. The article emphasizes the restrictive nature of the legislation and illustrates the importance placed on registration as a means of controlling the activities of churches, while denying that it in any way limits freedom of conscience.

[. . .] In our country citizens are guaranteed full realization of freedom of conscience, that is the right to confess or not to confess any religion, to hold or not to hold a religious world-view, to perform religious cults or conduct atheist propaganda. It is not by chance that Soviet legislation on cults is justifiably called legislation on freedom of conscience. It excludes any kind of constraint on man's conscience.

Soviet legislation on cults has been developed and refined simultaneously with the development of socialist democracy. The 'Regulations on religious associations in the Ukrainian SSR' were adopted by decree of the Presidium of the Supreme Soviet of the Ukrainian SSR on 1 November 1976. [. . .]

The present legislation on cults makes provision for questions about the registration of religious associations and the opening and closing of places of worship to be decided by a central body, the Council for Religious Affairs (CRA) attached to the USSR Council of Ministers. The 'Regulations' define the role and functions of the CRA attached to the Council of Ministers of the Ukrainian SSR, a state body which is one of the structural subdivisions of the CRA attached to the USSR Council of Ministers.

In the new legislation the principle of centralization in the exercise of control over the implementation of the legislation on religious cults is embodied in several articles.

The 'Regulations' state that believing citizens who have reached the age of 18 may, for the satisfaction of their religious needs, come together voluntarily into religious congregations, which are local associations of believing citizens of one and the same cult, denomination or movement.

A religious congregation or group of believers has the right to begin its activities only after the CRA attached to the USSR Council of Ministers has decided to register it.

Bourgeois propaganda and sectarian extremists, especially supporters of the schismatic Baptists, unregistered Christians of Evangelical Faith (Pentecostals) and some others, try to distort the true nature of registration, making it out to be a limitation on the rights of believers, on their freedom of conscience. [. . .]

What is the purpose of registration and what is its essence? The very act of registration means that the religious association takes upon itself the obligation to obey Soviet laws, placing itself at the same time under the protection of the law. In this way registration serves the interests of the believers themselves. Of course, it also corresponds to the interests of the state, in so far as it provides for the activity of registered congregations, and consequently, their members, within the framework of existing legislation. Thus the interests of believers who have formed associations are reinforced in the legislation on cults.

Believers have all the rights and conditions necessary for satisfying their religious needs to the full and for normal internal church activity. The legal establishment of these rights has the purpose not only of defining the limits of the organizational and ecclesiastical activity of religious associations, but also of guaranteeing believers the opportunity to realize in practice the principles of freedom of conscience.

Art. 11 of the 'Regulations' [corresponding to Art. 17 of the RSFSR law. *Ed.*] states that religious associations may engage only in activity directed towards the fulfilment of religious needs. Thus it is forbidden by law to create mutual aid funds, cooperatives, production associations or to use the property at the association's disposal for any purpose other than for satisfying the religious needs of the believers.

One should dwell also on Art. 17 of the 'Regulations'. It states that ministers of the cult may commence their activity only after they have been registered according to the established procedure. Their activities are limited to the place of residence of the members of the religious association which they serve, and to the location of the prayer premises of the association.

These regulations follow logically from the established procedure for registering religious associations with the state authorities. Their essence is that after registration both religious associations and their ministers of the cult come under the protection of Soviet legislation. In practice, unfortunately, there are some cases when ministers of the cult (presbyters, deacons and preachers) perform their duties without registration with the state authorities. In this way they are violating Soviet legislation on cults. It is necessary to eliminate these violations and not to allow them.

The 'Regulations' (Art. 20) indicate that religious associations may be removed from registration in the event of their violating the legislation on cults. The final decision on the removal of registration from a religious association, and on the closure of a church or any other prayer building, is taken by the CRA attached to the USSR Council of Ministers at the request of the executive committee of the regional *soviet* of people's deputies, and on the recommendation of the CRA attached to the Council of Ministers of the Ukrainian SSR. This approach to the matter makes a deep and all-round examination of each individual case possible and helps avoid mistakes.

Soviet legislation on religious cults clearly defines the procedure and reasons for removing religious associations from registration, and for closing prayer buildings and churches. Religious associations may be removed from registration for the following reasons: (*a*) gross violation of the legislation on religious cults; (*b*) failure of the religious association to observe the conditions of the agreement reached with the executive committee of the district *soviet* [for use of the building. *Ed.*] and (*c*) the collapse of the congregation.

The closure of prayer buildings and churches is allowed in two cases: (*a*) if the religious association using the prayer premises is removed from registration and (*b*) if the premises of the cult require to be demolished in the course of redevelopment of the area or if the building is unsafe.

In the latter case the believers may receive other premises for worship if available. It is appropriate to emphasize here that according to the legislation on cults all prayer premises, and also all property necessary for the conduct of the cult, whether made available to the believers of religious congregations under a contract, or acquired by them or donated to them, are the property of the state, and the executive committee of the district or city *soviet* of people's deputies is accountable for them. They are made available *gratis* to believers who have formed a religious congregation on the conditions and according to the procedure provided for by the contract (Arts. 28–9).

Soviet legislation guarantees free conduct of religious rites, provided they do not disturb public order and are not accompanied by infringements on the rights and health of citizens. At the same time the legislation does not permit the performance of religious rites or ceremonies, or the storage of any objects of the cult on the premises of state, cooperative or public enterprises, institutions or organizations (Arts. 22, 25).

The 'Regulations' stipulate that the performance of religious rites in the open air, outside the premises of the cult, may take place in each individual case only with the permission of the executive committee of the district or town *soviet* of people's deputies (Art. 25).

Soviet legislation lays down special legal norms which protect believers, ministers of the cult and religious associations from infringements of their legal rights. These norms cover responsibility for the hindrance of religious rites, provided the latter do not disturb public order and are not accompanied by infringements of the rights and health of citizens. Any kind of discrimination against believers or constraint on their conscience is forbidden by law.

As we can see, Soviet legislation guarantees all citizens full freedom to choose their attitude to religion, and it is a firm legal guarantee of freedom of conscience. At the same time it specifies that a citizen's adherence to one or other religious movement cannot serve as a reason for refusing to fulfil any civic obligation. 'Nobody', reads Art. 1 of the 'Regulations', 'may evade the fulfilment of his civic duties on the grounds of his religious convictions.' This requirement is entirely in accordance with the new Constitution of the USSR, in particular with Art. 59, which reads: 'The realization of rights and freedoms is indivisible from the fulfilment of his duties by a citizen', and also with the stipulations of Art. 39, which states that 'the enjoyment of rights and freedoms by citizens may not cause harm to the interests of society and the state, or to the rights of other citizens'.

It should be made clear that an absolute majority of ministers of the cult in the republic takes a consistently loyal position towards the Soviet state, and actively supports its policy and conducts religious activity within the framework of the law. The vast majority of rank and file believers conscientiously fulfils civic obligations, and alongside all Soviet people works actively and eagerly to fulfil the great plans of communist construction and the historic decisions of the XXV Congress of the CPSU.

Unfortunately, here and there in our republic violations of the legislation on the part of some ministers and believers still take place. These involve the luring of children and young people into participating in services, rituals and orchestras and into serving the clergy in church. Sometimes ministers of the cult try to teach religion to children.

The violations of the legislation also include such activities as missionary work, the interference of ministers of the cult in the financial affairs of the congregations, and the performance of rituals and also the repair of prayer premises in violation of the established procedure. The facts show that most violations of the legislation on cults result from inadequate knowledge of the legislation. At the same time one should not forget that Soviet laws provide for both administrative and criminal responsibility for violating the legislation on cults, the law on the separation of Church and state and school and Church, and for the infringement of the person and rights of citizens on the pretext of performing religious rites. [. . .]

Nobody has the right to ignore our laws, to evade the fulfilment of civic duties, to violate the procedures existing in the country, or to infringe the person and rights of other citizens. Every citizen of the USSR must unswervingly keep his constitutional obligations and the laws of our country, including the laws on religious cults.

DOCUMENT 4:
EXTRACTS FROM THE 1977 CONSTITUTION OF THE USSR

Article 6
'The Communist Party of the Soviet Union (CPSU) is the leading and guiding force of Soviet society and the nucleus of its political system, of all state and public organizations. The CPSU exists for the people and serves the people.

Armed with the Marxist-Leninist teaching, the Communist Party shall determine the general perspective of society's development, and the guideline of the internal and external policy of the USSR, give guidance to the great creative endeavour of the Soviet people and place their struggle for the triumph of communism on a planned, scientific basis.'
Article 25
'In the USSR a uniform system of education shall exist and be developed, which shall serve the communist education and cultural and physical development of young people, their training for work and social activity.'
Article 34
'Citizens of the USSR shall be equal before the law, irrespective of origin, social and property status, race or nationality, sex, education, language, attitude to religion, type or character of occupation, domicile or other particulars.

Equality of rights of citizens of the USSR shall be ensured in all fields of economic, political, social and cultural life.'

Article 52

'Freedom of conscience, that is the right to profess any religion or
not to profess any religion, to perform religious rites or to conduct
atheist propaganda shall be guaranteed for all citizens of the USSR.
Incitement of hostility and hatred on religious grounds shall be
prohibited.

The church in the USSR shall be separated from the state and
the school from the church.'

DOCUMENT 5:
CHRISTIAN CRITIQUE OF SOVIET DRAFT CONSTITUTION

*The following Appeal from the Christian Committee for the Defence of
Believers' Rights (CCDBR) in the USSR was addressed to L. I. Brezhnev, chairman of the Constitutional Commission which drew up the new
Soviet Constitution. The Draft Constitution was unanimously passed by
the Supreme Soviet of the USSR on 7 October 1977.*

Respected Chairman of the Constitutional Commission!

The Draft of the new Constitution of the USSR proclaims:

> 'A new historical community of people has been formed—the
> Soviet people. It is a society of high organizational capacity,
> ideological commitment and consciousness of the working
> people who are patriots and internationalists.'

Nevertheless, this society includes people of greatly differing
views, persuasions and beliefs. A significant part of it consists of
people of different religions, who wish to be and are loyal citizens
of the Soviet state, although in essence their outlook conflicts with
Marxism-Leninism.

Marxist-Leninist theory is the basis of the ideology of the CPSU
(Communist Party of the Soviet Union), the ruling party of the
USSR, membership of which is in principle *voluntary*. The building
of communism is the fundamental and ultimate aim of the CP and
its sympathizers. With the Marxist-Leninist theory, communism
appears as a society in which all the finest aspirations of mankind
will be realized, with the exception of religious ideals, the ideals
of the spiritual and moral unity of people with God, and with each
other in God. The published programme of the CPSU leaves no
doubt that, as far as present-day Party theoreticians understand the

position of communism and religion, with the approach towards communism, religion must be done away with. The Rules of the CPSU impose upon each member of the Party the duty: 'to lead a resolute struggle against the survivals of religion'. An anti-religious policy was and remains an integral part of the theory and practice of the CPSU, which is expressed *not only in atheistic propaganda*, which is being carried out by the Party and state organs using state, i.e. *public* resources. One of the manifestations of the anti-religious policy of the CPSU is the legal discrimination against religious organizations, which are established by believers:

a strict control of their lives by state organs,
deprivation of their rights as a juridical person,
and of the right to possess material property,
prohibition on charitable activities,
a ban on religious preaching and public worship, outside the prayer buildings,
a ban on the teaching of religion (with the exception of instruction of children by their parents and teaching in special schools),
a discriminatory policy of rejecting believers' petitions for the registration of a new community, for the opening of a new church.

Essential elements of religious life are either extremely limited or simply forbidden, under threat of criminal prosecution.

Thus, the strategy and tactics of the governing CPSU in the building of communism presuppose diverse forms of struggle with religion, through law, administration, and propaganda. The CPSU asserts in theory and realizes in practice the principle of the incompatibility of communism and religion.

The Draft of the New Constitution does not essentially change the legal position of religion in the USSR. Art. 52 of the Draft, which proclaims freedom of conscience, like Art. 124 of the previous Constitution, does not grant believers the freedom to preach (which the first Constitution of the RSFSR did guarantee). Art. 25 legalizes '*a uniform system of education, which is devoted to a communist upbringing*'.

This means that school curricula at all levels of education, from primary to higher schools, will in future be filled with anti-religious content. And pupils, regardless of their personal attitude towards religion, will be obliged to assimilate this material. This apparently also means that the teaching of religion will be pro-

hibited as before (with the exception of instruction of children by
their parents and teaching in special theological institutions).

But a particular fear is aroused in believers by that clause of the
Draft, where for the first time in Soviet history 'the building of a
communist (i.e. atheist, according to the authors of the Draft)
society' is declared, *by legislation*, to be the supreme goal not only
of the Party, but of the whole state:

> *'The Soviet state is a new type of state, the principal instrument in the*
> *building of communism.' 'The supreme goal of the Soviet state is the*
> *building of a classless communist (read: atheist) society.'*

Amongst the chief tasks of the state *'the education of the citizen of*
a communist society' is particularly indicated. A citizen of a *'communist*
society' from the point of view of the contemporary ideology of
the CPSU, is certainly *an atheist*.

The Constitution is the fundamental law of the state, having
binding power over all its citizens. With the acceptance of the
proposed Draft, all Soviet citizens, including millions of believers,
will be bound by legislation to participate in the building of a
totally godless society, which is completely unacceptable to a religious conscience. To a religious mind Art. 6 of the Draft is also
unacceptable; it states in particular that:

> *'The CP, armed with Marxism-Leninism, determines the general*
> *perspectives of the development of society . . . directs the great construc-*
> *tive work of the Soviet people, and imparts a planned, systematic and*
> *theoretically substantiated character to their struggle for the victory of*
> *communism.'*

A believer cannot agree with the Constitutional legalization of
compulsory godlessness for the whole of society. In fact, the
preamble and Art. 6 of the Draft set out the theses of the Party
Programme, which have now been elevated to the status of national law. Thus, the borderlines between the Party and the state
are obliterated once and for all, and the Soviet citizen's passport
becomes a communist's Party card. The Draft of the new Constitution turns the Soviet state, by a legal document, into *an ideocratic-*
totalitarian state.

If this draft is accepted, then in all seriousness believers
will face an agonizing question: can they, without prejudice
to their religious conscience, remain citizens of a state which
proclaims by law that national atheism is its goal?

'Render therefore unto Caesar the things which are Caesar's; and unto God the things that are God's'—such is the unalterable God-given principle for the relationship of the Christian to the state. This principle warns Christians against both extremes: against the anarchic rejection of state power, and against concessions to the state, in the event of excessive claims. Christianity has remained loyal to the state and its laws under all social and economic systems that have existed until now: slave-owning, feudal, capitalist and socialist. But whenever the state laws encroached upon the conscience of Christians, then Christians were obliged to violate them, even under threat of terrible torture and death.

We expect the Constitutional Commission to treat with understanding the problems which confront the religious conscience of believers in our country. We hope that our Appeal will be studied properly when the final text of the new Constitution is drawn up.

A possible way out of the legal crisis which is arising, is as follows:

1. The ruling Party excludes from its Rules the clause which obliges each member 'to lead a resolute struggle against the survivals of religion'.
2. It officially accepts the principle of the compatibility of communism and religion.
3. That the possibility, in principle, of religion existing with communism is included as a proposition in the text of the new Constitution of the USSR.

Members of the Christian
Committee for the Defence of
Believers' Rights in the USSR:

Gleb Yakunin
Varsonofi Khaibulin
Viktor Kapitanchuk

8 June 1977
Moscow

DOCUMENT 6:
EXTRACTS FROM THE CRIMINAL CODE OF THE RSFSR (RUSSIAN REPUBLIC)

Religious offences
Article 142. Violation of the laws on the separation of church and state and of school and church.

1 'is punishable by correctional tasks for a period not exceeding one year or by a fine not exceeding fifty roubles.

2 'The same actions committed by a person previously sentenced for violating the laws on the separation of church and state and of school and church, and likewise organizing activity directed at the commission of such actions are punishable by deprivation of freedom for a period not exceeding three years.'

Article 227. Infringement of the person and rights of citizens under the guise of performing religious rituals.

1 'Organizing or leading a group whose activity, carried on under the guise of preaching religious doctrines and performing religious rituals, is connected with causing harm to citizens' health or with other infringements of the person or rights of citizens, or with inciting citizens to refuse to do social activity or to fulfil civic obligations, and likewise with enticing minors into such a group, is punishable by deprivation of freedom for a period not exceeding five years or exile for the same period with or without confiscation of property.

2 'Active participation in the activity of a group such as described in the first part of this article, and likewise systematic propaganda directed at the commission of the acts described therein, is punishable by deprivation of freedom for a period not exceeding three years, or exile for the same period, or correctional tasks for a period not exceeding one year.'

[By a twist of penal law, article 209 in Ukraine can carry a sentence of five years imprisonment *followed* by five years exile.]

Under art. 142 it is an offence to organize any activity of an unregistered church and to teach religion to children (except one's own). Art. 227, introduced in 1959, was initially directed mainly at Pentecostals. It was soon, however, also applied to Baptists who left the officially recognized Church and has been applied to Christians of almost all denominations, and even to Buddhists. The essential features are 'causing harm to health' (frequently stated to result from speaking in tongues by Pentecostals) and 'inciting citizens to refuse to do social activity', for example, urging members not to take part in secular cultural activities.

Military offences

Article 80. Evasion of regular call to active military service

'is punishable by deprivation of freedom for a period of one to three years.'

Article 249. Evasion of military service by maiming or any other method.

(*a*) 'The evasion by a person in military service of performance of military duties by causing himself any kind of injury (maiming) or by malingering, forgery of documents or any other deception, or a refusal to perform military duties is punishable by deprivation of freedom for a period of three to seven years.

(*b*) 'The same acts committed in wartime or in a combat situation are punishable by death or by deprivation of freedom for a period of five to ten years.'

Refusal to be drafted into the armed forces is likely to bring an automatic conviction under art. 80, and the military authorities might subsequently repeat the call-up. Under art. 249 (*a*) refusal to swear the military oath (which is unacceptable to many Christians) can be construed as refusal to perform military duties, on the grounds that many duties cannot be performed by soldiers who have not sworn the oath. However, prosecution is not automatic and Christian soldiers are often transferred to units engaged in construction projects.

Political offences

Article 70. Anti-Soviet agitation and propaganda.

1 '. . . is punishable by deprivation of freedom for a period of six months to seven years, with or without additional exile for a period of two to five years, or by exile for a period of two to five years.'

2 'The same actions committed by a person previously convicted of especially dangerous crimes against the state . . . are punishable by deprivation of freedom for a period of three to ten years with or without additional exile for a period of two to five years.'

Article 190–1. Circulation of deliberately false concoctions, slandering the Soviet state and social order.

'. . . is punishable by deprivation of freedom for a period not exceeding three years, or by correctional tasks for a period not exceeding one year, or by a fine not exceeding one hundred roubles.'

Art. 70 is applied in cases where fundamental criticism has been made, for example of the USSR's record on human rights, or of the treatment of national minorities. Art. 190–1 is frequently applied to Christians who have written or spoken of persecution of the Church or been involved in the circulation of documents detailing violations of religious freedom and other human rights.

II.

The Orthodox Churches

(a) RUSSIAN ORTHODOX CHURCH

One of the chief aims of Lenin's 1918 decree on the separation of church and state was to ensure that the special privileges which had been granted to the Russian Orthodox Church since the tenth century should be abolished and that all religious denominations should henceforth be treated as equal before the law. In practice, however, there are still certain privileges accorded to the Orthodox Church not equally shared by other religious groups. There is a danger, however, that the splendour of a public display of ritual at home and the regular travel abroad of Orthodox dignitaries (usually young) may blind world public opinion to the realities behind this appearance.

Extensive documentation is now available, for example, about the nationwide enforced and illegal closure of churches during the latter part of Mr Khrushchev's regime (1960–64). Precise statistics on this are unobtainable, for we do not know for certain the number of open churches either before 1960 or now. However, the number of closures given by two young Orthodox priests resident in Moscow, Nikolai Eshliman and Gleb Yakunin, in a careful study of church–state relations during the early 1960s,[1] is ten thousand—or roughly half of all those which existed at the beginning of the Khrushchev period. An official anti-religious publication in Moscow[2] said later that the number of churches remaining open was as low as 7,500; this figure was repeated in another book published in 1971,[3] and in an official lecture given

[1] Open Letter to Patriarch Alexi, 21 November 1965; English in Michael Bourdeaux, *Patriarch and Prophets*, London, Macmillan, 1970 (reprinted Mowbrays 1975) pp. 194–221.
[2] *Propagandist's and Agitator's Handbook*, Moscow 1966, p. 149.
[3] E. I. Lisavtsev, *Critique of the Bourgeois Falsification of the Situation of Religion in the USSR*, Moscow, Mysl, 1971, p. 9.

in 1976.[4] Since 1964 this mass closure of churches has ceased, but despite hints that individual buildings have been reopened since then, the number is not substantial and there has been no return to the *status quo ante*.

It is quite certain that many other parishes have unsuccessfully tried to gain registration since 1964, despite the legal provision that any group of twenty people of the same denomination has the right to be granted a building for worship. Especially well-documented is the case of 1,500 believers in the city of Gorky, who applied in 1967 for the right to open a church. In a letter to Dr Eugene Carson Blake, then General Secretary of the World Council of Churches,[5] 36 of the petitioners state that in the whole of their city, with a population of 1,200,000, there are at least 120,000 Orthodox Christians. Yet they have between them only three small churches, all situated at a distance from the city centre and holding no more than 4,000 standing people altogether. They said that the provision of an extra church would help to relieve the dangerous overcrowding in the existing buildings. For months these petitioners received no answer whatsoever, and finally they were told that the existing churches were sufficient. The application was several times repeated in 1967–68 and finally in desperation the case was made known to the outside world. Subsequently five separate parish committees were formed, each of which has continued to make applications to register churches, but none has succeeded in receiving back any of the 37 churches in Gorky which were expropriated under Lenin and Stalin.

Orthodox believers of Naro-Fominsk, near Moscow, have been trying for forty years to have a church registered. They appealed in 1970 to the Soviet authorities (in a petition with 1,432 signatures) and their cause was taken up also by the civil rights leader (now in the West) Valery Chalidze, who is not a Christian. In 1979 information reached the West about a number of churches scattered over the western regions of the Soviet Union which have been trying repeatedly but unsuccessfully to register ever since they were forcibly closed under Khrushchev.[6] In a letter to Dr Philip Potter, Secretary-General of the World Council of Churches, Father Gleb Yakunin and Lev Regelson point out that registration

---

[4] Lecture in May 1976 by a deputy chairman of the Council for Religious Affairs, reported in *A Chronicle of Current Events*, no. 41; English in *Religion in Communist Lands* vol. vi, no. 1, p. 32.
[5] Published in the *Church Times*, London, 1 August 1969.
[6] See Document 12, p. 39.

reveals 'a fundamental drawback in Soviet legislation on religion: registration is understood not as an act of recognition but as an act of *sanction*, i.e. not as simple confirmation of the fact that a religious society exists, but as *permission* for it to exist.'[7]

The book *Patriarch and Prophets*[8] gives details of the closure at the beginning of the 1960s of most of the 69 monasteries and convents and of five of the eight theological seminaries.

During the early 1960s there were a number of cases of slander against Orthodox believers in the Soviet newspapers: it was common practice to accuse Orthodox believers (from archbishops down) of all kinds of debauchery and immorality. In the fifty-five years that such allegations have been made (with some intermissions), there has not been a single instance where the person slandered has been given the right of public reply. One of the most notable cases of such public slander occurred in 1960.[9] Archbishop Iov of Kazan was accused in the courts of financial dishonesty and of swindling the state of more than two million roubles income tax. If all the accusations were true, the sentence of three years was extremely mild, seeing that many people were shot for 'economic crimes' in the Khrushchev era. Presumably Archbishop Iov was released in 1963 and retired somewhere quietly. But in November 1967 the Holy Synod appointed him Archbishop of Ufa. Such an act would have been inconceivable if there had been any truth in the accusations. It virtually proves that the original accusations were a fabrication.

In many instances, the articles appear to have been written in order to prejudge a forthcoming trial and to whip up public sentiment against the accused. A striking example of this is an article which appeared in the leading Soviet weekly *Literaturnaya Gazeta* (Literary Gazette) in April 1977, called 'Freedom of Religion and the Slanderers'. It criticized, by name, at length, and in libellous terms, four of the best known Russian Orthodox activists: Father Dmitri Dudko, Father Gleb Yakunin, Lev Regelson and Alexander Ogorodnikov. The four held a press conference for foreign correspondents at which they disproved all the charges against themselves in detail—but their defence was not published in

---

[7] Letter of 6 March 1976; English in *Religious Liberty in the Soviet Union*, Keston College, 1976, p. 42.

[8] Michael Bourdeaux, London 1970, ch. 3; reprinted by Mowbrays, London & Oxford, 1975.

[9] *Izvestia*, 8 July 1960.

Literaturnaya Gazeta or anywhere else in the Soviet Union.[10] At the time, the article was taken as a declaration of intent to arrest the four, and this is what happened, even though nearly three years elapsed before the last of them, Father Dudko, was finally arrested.

In November 1967 and April 1968 members of the 'All-Russian Social-Christian Union for the Liberation of the People' were given long sentences of imprisonment. The group was not purely religious, but its aim was the Christianization of politics, culture and society. They have now served their sentences, except for the group's leader, Igor Ogurstov, who was sentenced to a total of twenty years, of which he has served thirteen. His time in prison and labour camp has undermined his health totally, so that his parents fear that he may not survive the remainder of his term.

In 1969 the prominent Orthodox layman, Boris Talantov, was imprisoned for three years and he died in prison hospital in January 1971. The lay church writer, Anatoli Levitin, was arrested soon after Talantov, and, after some legal confusion due to the fabrication of the case, sentenced to three years. He was released in the spring of 1973. However in September 1974, Levitin arrived in the West. Finding it impossible to continue his work in the Soviet Union, he was forced to leave his native land.

In 1974 Vladimir Osipov was arrested, and was later sentenced to eight years in labour camp. His 'crime' was editing the *samizdat* (self-published) journals *Veche* (the word means a village assembly in old Russia) and *Zemlya* ('earth' or 'land'); they were patriotic in content, with a religious theme, and Osipov specifically stated that their editorial policy was loyalty to the state. The roll-call of other Orthodox believers sent to labour camps, prisons and internal exile because of their Christian activities is, sadly, too long to give here.

Forcible incarceration of sane people in psychiatric hospitals because of their religious or political convictions has in recent years been acknowledged by competent western bodies as an all-too-common feature of Soviet life. Several Orthodox Christians have been subjected to such treatment. Still incarcerated at present, with no date set for their release, are, among others, Sister Valeriya Makeeva,[11] a nun from a convent forcibly disbanded under Khrushchev, Anatoli Ponamaryov, a 47-year-old layman from

[10] The full text of the article and the replies is given in English in Fr Gleb Yakunin and Lev Regelson, *Letters from Moscow*, ed. Jane Ellis, co-published in 1978 by Keston College and H. S. Dakin Company, San Francisco.

[11] See Document 11, p. 38.

Leningrad, and Vasili Shipilov, a former seminary student, who has been held in psychiatric hospitals since 1950.

One Russian Orthodox priest of whom much has been heard in the West recently is Father Dmitri Dudko.[12] From November 1973, after Saturday vespers in his Moscow church, he held question and answer sessions in which he dealt with the Christian faith and Christian living. This was a most unusual activity in present-day Russia, and attracted many people to the Church of St Nicholas. One person describes these sessions in this way:

> At Father Dmitri's discussion times I saw a tightly-packed crowd—the church could not hold them all. I saw people of all ages, nationalities and financial circumstances. From the numerous reactions of my friends, I know of the huge influence of these discussions. For many, they opened the way to a new, bright and hitherto completely unknown world. Judging by the questions people asked Fr. Dmitri, it is quite clear how vitally necessary his discussions were and how little known are the basic tenets of the Christian faith, to which people are now being so drawn—but where can they learn?[13]

However, such activity was not popular with the state authorities who, in turn, brought pressure on the church hierarchy. At the beginning of May 1974, Fr Dmitri was called to Patriarch Pimen and told to stop the question and answer sessions. He was then removed from his church. His parishioners continued to support him, however, expressing their dismay at his treatment in several appeals to the Patriarchate.

Father Dudko was sent to the parish of Kabanovo, 85 kilometres from Moscow, but was later abruptly removed from it and sent to Grebnevo, 35 km from Moscow but in an area closed to foreigners. Here he continued to preach vigorously, attracting people, especially young people, from all over the Soviet Union. His popularity led to increasing harassment from the authorities, and, finally, to his arrest on 15 January 1980.

Until recently, far less was known about the treatment of Orthodox prisoners than about Baptist prisoners, but recent accounts have shown that they are subjected to the same grinding regime

---

[12] See Document 7, p. 25.

[13] Open letter to Archbishop Pitirim from Igor Shafarevich, Soviet mathematician and member of Sakharov's Human Rights Committee, in defence of Fr Dmitri. Russian in *Russkaya Mysl'* 18 July 1974, p. 5; English translation in *Keston News Service*, no. 5, pp. 2–3.

of poor-quality, inadequate food, intense physical labour and lack of medical care that is the lot of all political and religious prisoners in the USSR. Occasional cases of brutality and death continue to be reported. Christians, additionally, face particular difficulty when it comes to maintaining a life of prayer and worship, as Yevgeni Pashnin-Speransky describes:

> a quiet corner where I could pray, away from the snores and groans of my fellow-prisoners. But in February 1973 I was punished for rising early and for being in the area of another barracks. My right to buy goods at the camp shop was withdrawn, along with my right to receive parcels, during March 1973. . . Several times I tried to take a little time off work time in order to devote it to prayer, but I was severely punished for absence from my place of work. How overjoyed I was when in January 1975 A. A. Petrov, A. I. Romanov and I succeeded in entering unobserved an empty refrigerated truck, which stood by a warehouse ready to be loaded. We threw ourselves on our knees on the icy floor and gave praise to Jesus Christ.[14]

It seems most likely that the sects which have gone into schism this century (such as the 'True Orthodox Church') and which the Soviet state has rendered illegal, have been worse treated than the Orthodox Church itself in recent years, though at the moment we lack concerted evidence. In 1977 ten True Orthodox women were reported to be in the same strict regime camp in Mordovia, all sentenced under article 70 of the Russian Criminal Code ('anti-Soviet agitation and propaganda') to terms of between 10 and 12 years combined labour camp and internal exile.

Where the early and mid-sixties saw the beginnings of a vigorous defence of the Orthodox faith against the atheist onslaught of the state, subsequent years have seen a refining of that process, with more detailed protests and complaints about specific issues which affect believers. Particularly significant have been the protest letters of Father Gleb Yakunin and Lev Regelson, addressed to both Soviet and Western bodies. Between 1974 and 1976 they wrote thirteen such letters, some separately some together, on a range of issues.[15] By far the most famous is their joint Appeal to Delegates of the Fifth Assembly of the World Council of Churches in Nairobi

---

[14] See Document 8, p. 27.
[15] Published in English in *Letters from Moscow* (see note 10 above).

in 1975.[16] It appealed for western Christians to demonstrate real support and concern for their brethren in countries where religion is persecuted, and gave several practical examples of how they could do so. Though not part of the Assembly's agenda, the appeal was nonetheless debated, to the great discomfiture of the official Russian Orthodox delegation. This was the first time that the WCC had ever openly debated the issue of religious persecution in the USSR.

Father Yakunin's name appears again as one of the founder-members of the Christian Committee for the Defence of Believers' Rights in the USSR, formed at the end of 1976. It stated that its aims were to defend the rights of religious believers if they were violated by state bodies, and to compile documentation on the subject.[17] To date, it has sent thirteen volumes of detailed documentation, a total of nearly 1300 pages, to the West, a major achievement for an unofficial body working under constant state pressure.[18] Father Yakunin was arrested on 1 November 1979, but his place was quickly filled by another priest, and the four-member Christian Committee is continuing its work.

Lev Regelson and Alexander Ogorodnikov have occupied leading positions in the work of the Christian Seminar, a discussion group for young Orthodox who have recently come to the faith. Founded in 1974 by Ogorodnikov, its members have endured constant KGB harassment since 1976, out of all proportion to their innocent activities. Ogorodnikov was arrested in November 1978, and Regelson took over the task of guiding and teaching the Seminar's young members, until he himself was arrested on 24 December 1979. Five other Seminar members have also been arrested.[19]

The support which the Christian Committee has received, and the continuation of the Christian Seminar, are witnesses to the growth of the numbers of people coming into the Orthodox Church, and of their commitment to it, despite the harsh retribution which many of them suffer.

[16] English translation in *Religion in Communist Lands*, vol. iv, no. 1, pp. 9–14, and also in *Letters from Moscow* (op. cit.)

[17] See Document 9, p. 31.

[18] The documents, in Russian with summaries in English, are available from Washington Research Center, 3101 Washington Street, San Francisco, California 94115, U.S.A.

[19] See Document 10, p. 33.

DOCUMENT 7:
DEFENCE SPEECH OF THE PRIEST FR DMITRI DUDKO

An accused person has a final defence speech; going away somewhere one bids farewell; any law grants this right. I also will avail
myself of the final defence speech.

As those who were present at my last discussion session will
remember, I announced that the Patriarch had forbidden me to
hold these discussions pending my conversation with him. However, as much as I tried to obtain an audience with the Patriarch,
he did not receive me, insisting through his secretary that I write
an explanatory note. I venture to quote this note.

To His Holiness Pimen,
Patriarch of Moscow and All-Russia,
from priest Dmitri Dudko
Church of St Nicholas
Preobrazhensky val, 25
Explanatory note

Your Holiness!

Fr Matthew, your secretary, asked me to write a note of ex-
planation, addressed to you personally, concerning my discussion times which I held in the church after Saturday vespers. As
Fr Matthew expressed it, these talks are for some reason being
called lectures. In the explanatory note, I was asked to give an
account of why and in what way I mentioned your name, the
type of questions discussed and why I did not obey the Dean
and the Rector of our church who asked me to stop these
discussions.

Bless me, Your Holiness!

The discussions took the form of sermons taking into account
the wishes of my parishioners. One could say the talks arose
spontaneously in accordance with the desire of believers. At the
beginning, I did not think that they would become interesting
and popular and attract so many people, and that people would
even come to listen from other parishes.

The influx of people from other parishes gave rise to some
diverse and penetrating questions, particularly that question in
answer to which I mentioned your name. Accusations were
hurled at you and at the name of the Church. I tried to defend

the Church and your name. How it turned out is not for me to judge.

Gossip began to grow around the talks, as the Dean and the Rector of our church told me. I did not pay any attention to their attempts to prohibit my discussions, because I did not consider it a ban, but advice, realizing that no one can prohibit sermons. If the discussions were to continue in the future (unfortunately I was informed that you had forbidden them pending my talk with you), I was already thinking of coming to Your Holiness for blessing on how I was to continue—because so many people had begun to gather that the church could not hold them all, and I was no longer in the position of satisfying by myself all the needs of the questioners.

Your Holiness!

I would be so bold as to approach you with my humble request. The discussions and the character of the questions showed that the Christian question is very important among our population. But sometimes, perhaps even often, the form of the sermons in contemporary church practice is so abstract and difficult as to be incomprehensible to the modern man. Apparently in my kind of talks those present have observed or found something they cannot understand and that is probably why such interest has been generated.

I would ask you, Your Holiness, in the future to bless not only me, but also other priests in the search for living forms of communion between pastor and congregation.

Of course, everything that is new contains something that is not successful and probably there was an element of failure in my discussions—something that by common effort could be put right in the future.

Your Holiness's obedient servant
Priest *D. Dudko*

After the explanatory note there followed an edict placing me at the disposal of Metropolitan Serafim, in other words sending me out of the city of Moscow into the outlying district. Puzzled as to how and why this had happened, I wrote a petition addressed to the Patriarch :

From your secretary Fr Matthew I received your edict transferring me to Metropolitan Serafim's jurisdiction. Several times I asked you to receive me. I was informed by your secretary that you, Your Holiness, refused me an audience. Therefore, not knowing what you have been told about me, and with what purpose and on what rights I am being transferred to the charge of Metropolitan Serafim, I assess all this as a measure designed to paralyse my activity as a priest, since I have violated no canonical law. In order to confuse the matter no further, I consider it necessary to retire from official church work.

I do so not because I do not want, let us say, to move out of Moscow, but because there is a measure of reprisal in the edict. How can I be given a guarantee that tomorrow Metropolitan Serafim will not issue an even more severe edict? It is obviously demanded of me that I cease active service as a priest. As the parishioners of our church will recall, this is not the first reprisal I have suffered: previously it came from the direction of the Procuracy (I was not removed thanks only to the intervention of believers), now it comes from the direction of the Patriarch, but there is only one source: an obvious intervention in internal church affairs on the part of certain persons who have no right to do so according to existing laws.

As then, I again appeal to public opinion—I have no other way. I am again prevented from serving in accordance with the laws of the Gospel and the church, and in obedience to my conscience as a priest. I am again flung out on the street, together with my small children, and for what reason?—because I want to be of use to people.

I request your prayers.

Priest *Dmitri Dudko*

DOCUMENT 8:
RUSSIAN ORTHODOX PRISONERS: CAMP CONDITIONS

Many samizdat *documents describing the treatment of Russian Baptists in prison have been received in the West. It is unusual to receive a document dealing with some of the problems facing Russian Orthodox believers in the camps. Below we print extracts from such a document entitled, 'The story of Ye.I.Pashnin-Speransky'.*

I find it very painful to write about what has been the theme of my earthly life, but seeing how those of my faith suffer torment in prisons and camps, I cannot remain silent. Between 1972 and 1975 officials of the MVD (Ministry of Internal Affairs) in camp

No. ZhKh 385/19, in the Mordovian Republic, repeatedly confiscated from me a prayer book, an Orthodox Calendar, the four Gospels (according to John, Luke, Matthew and Mark), and Metropolitan Makari's *Extracts from Orthodox Dogma*. When I asked why they continually confiscated the above-mentioned religious literature, and forbade the holding of services, an official at camp No. ZhKh 385/19, Vorobyev, replied at the end of May 1975, 'Prisoners are forbidden to possess literature of this type, even if it is handwritten'. He made no reference to any article of the law to substantiate his prohibition. On 10 June 1975 I felt compelled to begin a hunger-strike to demand the return of a handwritten prayer book, so that I could say prayers at the appropriate times. On 12 June 1975, the second day of the hunger-strike, a senior official of the camp, Kiselev, gave me back my prayer book and I broke off the fast. [. . .]

Two months after the first confiscation of my 'prohibited' Orthodox religious literature, in May 1973, my prayer book was again confiscated by the chief warder, Karkash. On my return from work I noticed that a handwritten Orthodox Calendar was missing from my belongings. It appeared that my possessions had been secretly searched and the Calendar had been taken by the chief warder. Secret searches of Christian prisoners in camp No. ZhKh 385/19 were a frequent occurrence, so that essential religious literature published by the Moscow Patriarchate had always to be hidden somewhere, or buried in the ground, so that the warders could not take it as often happened to me. [. . .]

At the end of November 1974, after I had suffered more privation than a weakened physical body can stand, the warder took my handwritten prayer book. As a result my health deteriorated. In the end the warder grew tired of confiscating my handwritten prayers. However, in practice it is impossible for a believer in a Soviet prison to make use of a prayer book, since the internal daily routine is so arranged that a believer cannot say the appropriate prayers without conflicting with the routine. I began by getting up at 6 a.m. (before reveille) so as to find a quiet corner where I could pray, away from the snores and groans of my fellow-prisoners. But in February 1973 I was punished for rising early and for being in the area of another barracks. My right to buy goods at the camp shop was withdrawn, along with my right to receive parcels, during March 1973. [. . .]

V. V. Kalinin used to pray in his brigade's storeroom just after reveille. But in October 1974 he was given 12 days in the cells 'for not attending physical exercises'. Kalinin is a classified invalid of the third group: his legs are swollen and ulcerated. On 13 October 1974 the door of the storeroom was padlocked by order of the camp administration, and Kalinin and I had to say our evening prayers out on the frozen autumn ground (on other days it would be damp), beneath the open sky and amid the dank irksome wailing of the wind; the stench from the latrines (three metres away from where we prayed) filled our noses so that we could hardly breathe. To avoid this unpleasantness we moved nearer to the bath-house, where Kalinin laid a sheet of plywood on the ground and used another as a shield from the wind and from the prying eyes of vigilant informers. And there we began to read our prayers.

Orthodox believers tried to pray behind the barracks in the angle of the wall, but warders found them and forbade them to meet together on the basis of Order No. 20 of the USSR Ministry of Internal Affairs. They were made to disperse to the living quarters: 'Otherwise you will be punished'. That would mean losing shop privileges, parcels, visits—or the cells. But how could they disperse, when Orthodox prayers are in fact intended for corporate use, for reading together; do they not begin, 'Our Father . . . forgive us our trespasses . . .' and so on. We had to divide into groups of two or three and slip behind the barracks, pretending to have a conversation but in fact to say prayers in an undertone so that watching informers would not realize that we were praying and report to the administration, who, in such circumstances, would immediately drive the believers away. On the decision of a priest, we began praying with heads covered, only removing the covering at the moment of making the sign of the cross. Orthodoxy forbids prayer with covered heads, but the administration of camp ZhKh 385/19 created conditions for believers such that one or the other had to go: either prayer, or conformity with this outward form. The situation remains so to this day. [. . .]

Several times I tried to take a little time off during work time in order to devote it to prayer, but I was severely punished for absence from my place of work.

How overjoyed I was when in January 1975 A. A. Petrov, A. I. Romanov and I succeeded in entering unobserved an empty refrigerated truck, which stood by a warehouse ready to be loaded. We threw ourselves on our knees on the icy floor and gave praise to Jesus Christ. But such moments of joy were few and far between during our life in captivity. They are imprinted on our memories, as one remembers the sight of a living flower in a patch of melted snow, if one has ever seen such a thing. Such a flower in the melting snow of my life was A. A. Petrov—a man who bore on his shoulders much human vileness. Praise be to Jesus Christ, who has in his flock such Christians as A. A. Petrov. [. . .]

Believers are not allowed to come together for festive meals. When we do gather nevertheless, as we did on Easter Sunday, 4 May 1975, warders arrived demanding that we disperse immediately. On 4 May 1975 the commandant of camp ZhKh 385/19, R. K. Akmaev, the programme administrator, Shein, and the head of ITK (Corrective Labour Colony) 17, Zinenko, summoned me to the office and there, among other humiliations, Akmaev called me 'scum' in the presence of the other officers named; and then, alarmed at my complaints, he sent me to the cells for 14 days on bread and water, where once in two days they gave me half a basin of watery soup and a small ladle of watery porridge, which in the language of the MVD is called hot food. So, by order of the servants of the MVD, our holy days are turned into humiliation and suffering.

If by any chance a holy day falls on a rest day, the camp administration declares that day a working day, and believers are punished if they fail to go to work that day. [. . .]

It was impossible to obtain official Orthodox literature, and that which arrived by unofficial means was rapidly confiscated by the administration.

Thus, on 20 February 1975, the *Acts of the Apostles* was taken from me. In 1971 Yu. Khramtsov was sent to Vladimir prison for three years for resisting the confiscation of a Gospel. We were forbidden to receive even the *Journal of the Moscow Patriarchate* because 'the Church is separated from the state'. Decree No. 20 of the USSR Ministry of Internal Affairs, which allows prisoners to obtain and possess literature published in the USSR, does not extend to believers because the Church is a 'private organization'. Moreover, religious literature published by the Moscow Patriarchate in the Soviet period is immediately confiscated from believers. Thus the believer, G. G. Superfin, was put in solitary confinement by the administration of the Vladimir prison on 22 January 1976 because he did not want to give up his Bible, prayer book and three copies of the *Journal of the Moscow Patriarchate*, published in 1970 by the Moscow Patriarchate under the supervision of the USSR Council of Ministers. When Superfin was out exercising, the prison administration took the forbidden literature from among his belongings without provocation. This led Superfin to go on a prolonged hunger-strike. On the third day of his fast he weighed 45 kilograms. He continued to fast for 35 days—from 22 January until 26 February. To the numerous protests and complaints made by political prisoners in the prison about this matter, the Assistant Procurator for the Vladimir district, I. F. Sychugov, replied (No. 4/53 of 13 February 1976, 17 February 1976 and 25 February 1976): 'the action of the prison administration is lawful'. An identical reply was received from the head of the UITU (Administration of Corrective Labour Establishments) of the Vladimir district Soviet's executive committee, I. P. Kapkanov (No. 9/12–11–259, 261 of 13 February 1976).

The legal adviser to the Council for Religious Affairs attached to the USSR Council of Ministers, V. A. Vorobyev, replied on 22 March 1976 (No. 636a): 'Please tell prisoner Pashnin that his *thirteenth complaint* has been sent to the appropriate department of the Ministry of Internal Affairs of the USSR'. The words 'thirteenth complaint' were underlined with a black wax crayon. It is not possible to complain about the lawlessness of the MVD men and of the procurators to the church hierarchy, since such complaints would immediately be confiscated. To use one of the limited private letters allowed (as the commandant of camp OD-1/st.2, Zavyalkin, explained to me on 4 February 1976) is not permitted, since it is forbidden to mention anything about conditions in personal letters. Again, letters on religious subjects are often confiscated for a trumped-up reason—'suspicious content'.[. . .]

DOCUMENT 9:
FOUNDING STATEMENT OF THE CHRISTIAN COMMITTEE FOR THE DEFENCE OF BELIEVERS' RIGHTS IN THE USSR

On 27 December 1976 the Christian Committee for the Defence of Believers' Rights (CCDBR) in the USSR was founded by three members of the Russian Orthodox Church—Fr Gleb Yakunin, hiero-deacon Varsonofi Khaibulin and Viktor Kapitanchuk. The following Declaration, issued by the founding members of the CCDBR, describes the aims of this Committee.

It is the inalienable natural right of every man to believe in God and to live in accordance with his belief. In principle, this right is acknowledged in the Basic Legislation of the USSR Soviet State Constitution. However, in practice, the principle of freedom of conscience proclaimed in the Constitution comes up against considerable difficulties as regards the attitude to religion of a government which is constructing a non-religious society. This attitude is expressed not only in the character of existing legislation, but also in the violation by the state administrative authorities of even those rights which believers legally possess. Religious believers form a significant proportion of the population in our country, and a normalization of their legal position is vitally necessary for the state, since it proclaims itself to be lawful and wholly representative.

Because of this, we considered it our Christian and civil duty to form the Christian Committee for the Defence of Believers' Rights in the USSR.

At present, the bishops of the Russian Orthodox Church and the leaders of other religious organizations do not concern themselves with the defence of believers' rights, for a variety of reasons. In such circumstances, the Christian community has to make the legal defence of believers its own concern.

The Committee's aim is to help believers to exercise their right of living in accordance with their convictions. The Committee intends:

1. To collect, study and distribute information on the situation of religious believers in the USSR.
2. To give legal advice to believers when their civil rights are infringed.
3. To appeal to state institutions concerning the defence of believers' rights.
4. To conduct research, as far as this is possible, to clarify the legal and factual position of religion in the USSR.
5. To assist in putting Soviet legislation on religion into practice.

The Committee has no political aims. It is loyal to Soviet laws. The Committee is ready to cooperate with social and state organizations, in so far as such cooperation can help in improving the position of believers in the USSR.

The Committee is made up of members of the Russian Orthodox Church. For centuries, Orthodoxy was the state religion in our country. Orthodox churchmen often allowed the state to use forcible methods to restrict the religious freedom of other denominations. As we acknowledge that any use of compulsion against people on the grounds that they are not Orthodox or belong to a different faith is contrary to the Christian spirit, we consider it our

especial duty to take the initiative in defending the religious freedom of all believers in our country, regardless of denomination.

We ask our fellow Christians to pray that God may help us in
our human frailty.

Members of the Christian Committee for the Defence of Believers'
Rights:
Gleb Yakunin,
priest
Varsonofi Khaibulin,
hiero-deacon
Viktor Kapitanchuk,
secretary of the Committee

Address: V. A. Kapitanchuk,
Sevastopolsky Prospekt 61, kv. 4,
Moscow.

27 December 1976

DOCUMENT 10:
SHORT LIST OF REPRESSIVE MEASURES CARRIED OUT DURING
THE PAST YEAR AGAINST THE SEMINAR ON PROBLEMS OF THE
RELIGIOUS RENAISSANCE (SEMINAR FOUNDED BY
A. OGORODNIKOV)

30 April 1978, Easter Day
Redkino, Kalinin Region. Seminar house surrounded by 10 local
militia-officers. A. Ogorodnikov, the house-owner, detained and
released only after militia informed that Seminar members had
given up hope of getting to the Easter service.
21 May 1978
Smolensk. Search of Tatyana Shchipkova's flat. Following members of Seminar detained for duration of search: Alexander Ogorodnikov, Yelena Kashtanova, Viktor Popkov, Tatyana
Shchipkova. Materials related to journal *Obshchina* confiscated.
21 May 1978, night
Vyazma, Smolensk Region. Sergei Yermolaev, member of Seminar, taken off Smolensk–Moscow train and detained until 10 a.m.
Two typewriters confiscated.
End of May 1978
Smolensk. Tatyana Shchipkova seized and taken to Smolensk

KGB. Warned that she was engaging in anti-Soviet activities. Told that she would risk trial if she continued them.
Beginning of June 1978
Smolensk. Tatyana Shchipkova dismissed from her job as teacher at pedagogical institute.
20 June 1978
Smolensk. Yelena Kashtanova, member of Seminar, expelled from third year of pedagogical institute (modern languages faculty).
End of June 1978
Smolensk. Viktor Popkov, member of Seminar, summoned to Smolensk KGB. Told that his participation in the Seminar and the meetings themselves were considered to be anti-Soviet activity. He would risk trial if he continued this activity.
3 July 1978
Smolensk. Alexander Shchipkov (Tatyana Shchipkova's son), member of Seminar, expelled from fourth year of pedagogical institute (modern languages faculty).

His wife, Lyuba Shchipkova, a student in the same group, told by dean of institute that she could continue studies only if she went over to the external department of another institute 'of her own accord'. (In August 1978 she transferred to the external department of Kolomensk Pedagogical Institute).
7 July 1978
Redkino, Kalinin Region. Secret search of Seminar house during A. Ogorodnikov's absence. Nothing taken, only turned over. Those responsible got into the house through a window.
Autumn 1978
Redkino, Kalinin Region. Observation point set up opposite Seminar house; observation and following of all members and guests of Seminar; operations cars posted near house; militia squads attempt to get into house without search-warrants. Those refused admission by owner make unsuccessful attempts to break down door.
October 1978
Redkino, Kalinin Region. Official refusal of A. Ogorodnikov's request for confirmation of individual peasant-worker status (i.e. someone living off his own plot of land).
25 October 1978
Leningrad. At a session of the specialized Academic Council of the USSR Academy of Sciences Institute of Linguistics Tatyana Shchipkova deprived of her academic status as Doctor of Philological Sciences 'for activities incompatible with the calling of a

Soviet academic'. This activity could be observed in the classes in which she gave students information about the history of the New Testament and of Christianity.

1 November 1978
Smolensk. Alexander Shchipkov called up for army service, forcing him to leave his wife and 10-month-old baby without means of subsistence.

17 November 1978
Redkino, Kalinin Region. Alexander Ogorodnikov and Tatyana Kolesnikova, members of Seminar, detained by local militia. Kolesnikova (17 years) sent to special juvenile reception centre in Kalinin; released on arrival of mother, who had been summoned.

Same day A. Ogorodnikov went to Kalinin to register for a job, about which he had been given preliminary agreement. The following two days were holidays.

20 November 1978
Redkino, Kalinin Region. Alexander Ogorodnikov, founder of young Christian Seminar, arrested.

Arrest carried out on platform of Redkino Station when Ogorodnikov was setting out to Kalinin to register his job. No heed was taken of his explanations to the militia-officers or request that they accompany him to Kalinin.

As stated by A. Ogorodnikov's lawyer at the trial, the time allotted him in which to find employment ran out on 22 November.

A. Ogorodnikov was presented with the following charge: the leading of a parasitic and anti-social type of life.

December 1978
Redkino, Kalinin Region. A. Ogorodnikov's father, resident of Chistopol, Tatar ASSR, summoned. Insistent demands made by Solovev, head of local militia department (investigator in Ogorodnikov's case), that his son's house be sold.

10 January 1979
Konakovo, Kalinin Region. Trial of A. Ogorodnikov. Only relatives of accused admitted into courtroom.

Sentence: one year's imprisonment in strict-regime camp with exemption from heavy physical labour (A. Ogorodnikov has had his spleen removed).

Sent to camp in Komsomolsk-on-Amur (two-month transit period).

End of January 1979

Sergei Yermolaev, member of Seminar, arrested on charge of malicious hooliganism.

According to the information received, he and his friend Igor Polyakov (also arrested) made critical remarks about the Soviet government while travelling on the underground.

Subjected to psychiatric examination. Up to present time (end of August) held in custody pending trial.

At time of arrest Sergei Yermolaev was 19 years old.

10 February 1979

Operations squad of No. 60 Moscow district militia division (two uniformed militia-officers and more than ten vigilantes in civilian clothing without armbands) broke into the flat where the regular meeting of the Seminar was being held. All those at the meeting were detained at the militia department until midnight.

The raid was carried out 'on suspicion of a meeting of a band of thieves'. Each detainee was made to give a statement. The religious literature confiscated has not yet (end of August 1979) been returned.

2 March 1979

Moscow. Opening of criminal proceedings against Tatyana Shchipkova on a charge of hooliganism during the raid of the operations squad on 10 February 1979.

March–April 1979

Moscow. Questioning of seminar members on 10 February as witnesses in the case of T. Shchipkova.

April 1979

Moscow. Summoning to Moscow and questioning of T. Shchipkova as accused in hooliganism case.

Prohibited from leaving Smolensk, T. Shchipkova charged with striking a vigilante. Awaiting trial.

End of May 1979

Moscow. Yelena Kolesnikova (17 years) dismissed from post as librarian.

June–July 1979

Moscow. Lieutenant-Colonel A. D. Shilkin, Head of KGB Church Department, held three 'preventive talks' with the mother of Yelena and Tatyana Kolesnikova. Various charges levelled at Seminar members.

July 1979

Kalinin. Publication in newspaper *Kalinin Truth* of article entitled

'Why Ogorodnikov needs his plot of land' containing charges against the Seminar.

July 1979

Kalinin. Preventive talk at town KGB with two young artists who had attended Seminar meetings.

1 August 1979

Leningrad. Vladimir Poresh, co-founder of Seminar, arrested.

Charge: distribution of hand-written anthology *Obshchina-2*, containing 'slanderous fabrications defaming the Soviet State system'.

Searches carried out in connection with this case at same time:

1. ul. Matrosa Zheleznyaka, d. 17, kv. 70 (where Poresh is registered).

2. prospekt imeni Morisa Toreza, d. 33, kv. 55 (where Poresh's wife is registered).

119 items, including religious and liturgical literature, personal correspondence, theology and philosophy books, confiscated during these searches.

3. flat of Leningrad poet Oleg Okhapkin.

4. Nikolai Yepishev's flat.

5. Vladimir Lazutkin's flat: from 26 July to 1 August (while he and his family were away) his flat was opened and the materials and books listed in the protocol of the search were confiscated.

92 items confiscated.

A list of books which the search did not uncover was included in the previously compiled protocol.

1 August 1979

Leningrad. Oleg Okhapkin and Nikolai Yepishev summoned for questioning as witnesses in the case of V. Poresh.

1 August 1979

Moscow. Searches of flats of Seminar members in connection with the *Obshchina-2* case:

1. Tatyana Lebedeva's flat, where Seminar meetings had been held in the preceding months (70 items confiscated).

2. Vladimir Burtsev's flat (an old notebook and postcard in a post-box were found in the deserted flat and included in the protocol).

6 August 1979

Leningrad. Vladimir Lazutkin questioned as witness.

10 August 1979

Search of Pavel Kulagin's flat. He had attended Seminar meetings.

13 August 1979

Leningrad. Pavel Kulagin summoned as witness in connection with

V. Poresh's case.

Several days after the arrest V. Poresh's case was handed over to the KGB.

The investigator in charge of the case is Vasily Viktorovich Cherkesov.

(Compiled 15 August 1979)

DOCUMENT 11:
ORTHODOX NUN SENT TO PSYCHIATRIC HOSPITAL

To Professor Peter Berner, Secretary-General of the World Psychiatric Association, from Viktor Nikolayevich Cheverev (address: Moscow, V-218, ul. Kedrova, dom 16, korpus 3, kv. 2).

Declaration

I ask you personally, Secretary-General, and your organization to pay urgent and serious attention to the monstrous psychiatric persecution being carried out against my cousin, Valeriya Zoroastrovna Makeeva, born in 1929 in Novocherkassk and now resident in Moscow, I–221, Zarevy Proezd, dom 5, korpus 96.

She was first subjected to psychiatric persecution in 1949, when she was arrested by the MGB and, on the instructions of the authorities, labelled mentally ill by the forensic-psychiatric doctors of Serbsky Institute. The diagnosis given was 'schizophrenia'. She was sent to the notorious Kazan 'special' (special psychiatric hospital), where she spent more than four years.

In 1972, again in Moscow, Makeeva was once more subjected to persecution at No. 5 psychiatric hospital (Stolbovaya), where she was held for seven months for making articles used in religious worship (Orthodox prayer books and belts embroidered with Psalm 91). In 1975 she was again sent to prison in Alexandrov, Vladimir Region; this time she was ruled not responsible and held for five months. Finally, on 15 June 1978 Makeeva was arrested by the Moscow authorities on a second charge of making psalm-belts. The Serbsky Institute forensic-medical examination again ruled her not responsible and gave a diagnosis of 'psychopathy accompanied by personality change'. Schizophrenia was excluded, because she admitted and demonstrated to the doctors that she had previously pretended to be mentally ill; all this, of course, was due to circumstances and contrived with the aim of avoiding persecution from the civic authorities for the manufacture of home-made church equipment, forbidden in this country. The Serbsky Institute made the following recommendation: Makeeva is ruled not responsible and diagnosed 'psychopathic'; she is not socially dangerous, but requires treatment in a special hospital.

She is being held at present in Butyrski prison hospital (institution IZ-48/2). Back at the beginning of her sentence Makeeva wrote me a letter from prison saying that this time she would rather be ruled responsible and sent to prison than go into psychiatric hospital, which she knew would mean either certain death or complete mutilation, since she was physically very ill. Makeeva is a 'servant of the cult', that is, an Orthodox nun belonging to a registered Orthodox community in Zhitomir in the Ukraine. She has relatives abroad in Mexico and England.

I urgently implore you, Mr Berner, the Secretary-General, and your world organization, to intervene as soon as possible in any way you can to save my cousin, Valeriya Makeeva, from an abhorrent slow death from psychiatric abuse in a special hospital. She is not mentally ill at all—only physically. This is the opinion of psychiatrists who know her, as well as myself and her relatives. In the near future, probably this May, a trial is due to take place in Moscow at Kirov District People's Court.[1] Something terrible awaits her. I implore you, please intervene.

24 February, 1979

Viktor Nikolaevich Cheverev

DOCUMENT 12:
CHURCH DESTROYED DESPITE VILLAGERS' PROTESTS

Rovno region, Sarny district, Zanosychi village.

Unyielding stronghold of Russian Christianity in Western Ukraine. Soviet authorities extremely concerned.

In 1910 the villagers of Zanosychi built themselves a church; believers throughout the neighbouring districts used to come to it to worship God. The storm of 1917 came and went, civil war swept the country, and still the church stood as before, attracting the prayerful to its sanctuary. The people of Western Ukraine, finding themselves under Soviet power, had enormous difficulty in res-

---

[1] Makeeva was tried on 12 April 1979 and sentenced to indefinite detention in a psychiatric hospital on the basis of an examination which found her 'psychopathic' (ed.).

toring the church. The Soviet authorities were indifferent to its fate. The Second World War went by, the Germans arrived and left again, leaving the church intact. Then, during the post-war years the Zanosychi church began to need repair-work. There was no priest and, consequently, no church hierarchy. The authorities did not respond to the parishioners' request for restoration work to be carried out. But Christ's flock were consumed with zeal for God. They could not rest while the church remained in a state of neglect. The news travelled from house to house and the funds needed for the repairs were collected. Appeals were made to the authorities, who wavered: what would the Sarny district committee say? The head of the atheist cult replied: 'Forbid the restoration of the Orthodox church.' Soviet power had not come in order that Christians might lead a carefree life. But the parishioners of Zanosychi and the neighbouring villages decided not to surrender. 'More and more people must obey God.' They began to carry out the repairs on the church themselves and to decorate the iconostasis. They painted the picture of God's house with especial diligence. When their work was completed, despite not having a priest, the hearts of the Orthodox fold were filled with reverence and tenderness. But the Antichrist was prowling in search of Christian joy no less assiduously, and a secret conspiracy of demonic forces determined the following. One night the church was burgled and when God's children came next to church it was completely empty. All the ornaments and decorations had been broken or stolen, and the windows were shattered. But the enemies of Christ did not stop there.

A few nights later the authorities drove an enormous tractor up to the church. It burrowed and rumbled and could not go about its work quietly. The driver did his best to demolish the old building, manoeuvring the tractor here and there, wherever he could. The parishioners ran up to see what the noise was and chased away the nocturnal murderer of the Orthodox faith. In the morning the whole neighbourhood poured out of their houses. The women wept and shook their fists towards the village *soviet* (council). The men stood in stern silence when they saw the bandits' claims on their souls. The Zanosychi villagers set up a round-the-clock watch around the church. For over a year they took it in turns, night and day, to safeguard their favourite gathering-place. Despite not having a priest, they went to their prayer house regularly, praying for God's intervention. Thus passed the summer and winter. The parishioners' zealous conduct annoyed the atheist thieves, who decided to burn the church down. This was the third night the devil's servants tried to carry out their villainous scheme. The villagers watched with astonishment as a fire-engine hurtled up, sirens wailing: where was the fire? But the firemen had business of a different kind to carry out. They poured a highly flammable liquid around the church and would have set light to it, had the parishioners not rushed up to surround the church and cried out in a chorus: 'We will not give in! If the church burns, we burn with it!' The arsonists made vain attempts to break them up. Those who were dragged away were replaced by new supporters. The Zanosychi parishioners stood firm by their prayer house.

When they saw this, the district authorities resorted to cunning. A meeting of the *kolkhoz* (collective farm) management was held and a decision passed. 'In view of the shortage of grain-storage space, the Zanosychi church is to be converted into a grain storehouse.' Ivan Pavlovsky, the chairman of the *kolkhoz*, and Pavel Varenich, the Party organizer, announced to the parishioners that their church, God's house, was to be taken from them in order to store grain. The people were shaken and offended. They decided unanimously not to go out into the fields or to the farms to work for the *kolkhoz*. The hungry cattle, left for a long time without food, sent up such a pitiful lowing that the local authorities were shocked. Everyone went on strike; even the children refused to go to school. The authorities were seized with panic; the cattle could be heard as far away as the district centre. The chairman was summoned, but he simply shrugged his shoulders. He was sent to reason with the people, but they said: 'We will not return to work until you have cleaned up our holy place.' They were obliged to give way. The church was freed. And once again the Zanosychi parishioners stood firm by their prayer house.

The authorities were enraged. And with good reason. The Soviets had total power in their hands, but still these Orthodox refused to surrender.

Spring arrived. It was Easter 1979. The people were getting ready for the Easter festivities. Although there was no priest in Zanosychi, the people went to pray at the church. The Easter vigil took place undisturbed. But dark storm-clouds were gathering overhead. Four days after the vigil Pavlovsky and Varenich hatched a crafty plot. They sent all the residents to another village, ostensibly to help with the ducklings, and padlocked all the children in the school. A bucket was put in each classroom so that they would not need to go out to the toilet. On 25 April 1979, at approximately 12 a.m., five busloads of militia and two trucks drove up to the church. After cordoning it off, they began to tear the church down, starting at several places at once. With their hooters blaring, the trucks knocked down the Orthodox architecture.

The deceived parishioners returned wailing to Zanosychi and, forming a circle around the church, demanded that Satan's work be stopped. The militia twisted their arms mercilessly. Distress and horror swept through the entire village. The communists had done something not even the Nazis had done, and during peace-time as well. It was a battle between the mountain serpent and the unarmed peasants. In the morning, under the command of the Sarny district procurator, the local authorities set fire to the church. The charred remains smoked, while the people wept. But even barbarity such as this was powerless to quell the people's zeal for God. With renewed fervour they journeyed from the remotest areas to pray to God at the smouldering ruins. They wound cloths and coloured ribbons around the nearby pine-trees in order to create a homely, reverential atmosphere around the holy place. The burnt church drew the attention of Christians even more than before and people came to see it in great numbers. The story of the vandalism perpetrated by the communists aroused indignation far and wide, and people flowed in from distant villages, filling the local houses. There were at least twenty guests staying in practically every single house. They had come for the intercessions, and in the morning, although there was no church, they went to the site of Zanosychi's Golgotha. Following the district procurator's instructions, the authorities carried out one malicious raid after another, in an attempt to disperse the believers. Then an order was given to prohibit entry to and exit from Zanosychi. People on foot or in cars were stopped and turned back. Those who had been to Zanosychi began to grow curious: was it true that the communists committed an act of such barbarity? The smouldering ruins of the desecrated house of God were proof enough. People who had travelled long distances decorated every branch and every twig at the site of the profaned holy place. The authorities could not find any way of stopping the pilgrims. Then they decided to cut down the pines on which decorations had been hung. They searched high and low for someone from Zanosychi or a neighbouring village who could do the job, but even the atheists refused. Finally, they found a prisoner serving a fifteen-year sentence and offered to release him if he cut down the pines.

The criminal inquired further into the matter and proved to be less of a criminal than the authorities, who were re-educating him: 'I cannot. My conscience would not allow it. There are so many believers here. I would be offending them!'

A fortnight later they found someone else—a hardened alcoholic. He agreed and, guarded by militia, started chopping down the old pines with an axe. Scattering needles, they fell like people under the executioner's axe. The felled pines stretched throughout the forest. 'There,' thought the devil's brood, 'there won't be anyone praying there now.' But the Christian soul is made of sterner stuff, and people flowed in from all over the area to decorate the pine stumps, their enthusiasm even greater than before. They placed ornaments on them and wound cloths around them, watering the destroyed holy place with their tears. The authorities were filled with fury. They called yet another meeting and passed a decision; bulldozers were brought in, the stumps dug out, a great pit dug and, on orders from above, everything buried in it: the stumps and everything that might remind people that a church had once stood there.

Four little pine-trees were left. People still come, crying and weeping, to the site of the old church and pray there as before. No one has cut down the little pines and it is easy to see why. The evil axe-wielder, who felled the sacred pines, went mad before the villagers' very eyes. He is often to be seen running through the forest gathering moss. 'What's up with you, sick man?', people ask him. The poor unfortunate puts the moss next to his breast and cries out: 'They're baking me, they're baking me!' Neither did the Antichrist, the procurator, escape punishment. A strong, healthy man, he died that same year. Nobody rejoices over the fact that the souls of the godless descend to Hell, but for the living this is a sign that the holy places of our Lord should not be touched.

The shameful authorities continue to search for ever more ways of forbidding the faith, but Orthodox Russia lives on and will do so as long as the devout carry on serving the Lord as fervently as in the Rovno region. Their hearts have become a temple for the Lord, and there is no hellish power capable of destroying such a temple.

Zanosychi village, Sarny district, Rovno region, Ukraine.
The parishioners of Zanosychi Church.

(b) GEORGIAN ORTHODOX CHURCH

During the nineteenth century the Georgian Church was completely integrated into the Russian Church and largely russified. After the 1917 revolution its status as an autocephalous Orthodox Church was restored, though strong links with the Russian Church remained. In 1972 a campaign against corruption in Georgia was inaugurated by new Party Secretary Shevarnadze and the investigations revealed corruption in the Orthodox Church as well as in the wider society. The abuses, which followed the uncanonical election of Catholicos-Patriarch David in April 1972, were carefully documented by a legal official, David Koridze, who submitted a report to the Central Committee of the Communist Party in Georgia on 19 March 1973. The exposure of the involvement of state officials by Koridze led, however, not to dismissals or reprimands, but to a cover-up. His report circulated and was backed up by documents by church members, one of whom, Valentina Pailodze was arrested in March 1974 and sentenced to 1½ years' imprisonment for 'slandering the Soviet state and social system'. Koridze himself was forced to retire early.[1]

Considerable looting of church treasures had taken place and those responsible were not removed from office. The situation changed after the death of Patriarch David in November 1977 and the election of Patriarch Ilya II, a churchman widely respected in his own church and abroad. Corrupt clergy were sacked, a number of undesirable bishops removed, and all the episcopal vacancies filled. Finally, Metropolitan Gaioz (Keratishvili/Patriarch David's right-hand man) was brought before a Soviet court for theft of church valuables and sentenced to 15 years' imprisonment.[2] The activity of the church has been revitalized, though the number of

[1] See Peter Reddaway, 'The Georgian Orthodox Church: Corruption and Renewal', *Religion in Communist Lands*, vol. iii, nos. 4–5, July–October 1975, pp. 14–23.
[2] *Keston News Service*, no. 79, 16 August 1979, p. 6.

44

seminary students is still limited by the authorities. Permission has been obtained for the reopening of two monasteries.[3]

DOCUMENT 13:
'ON THE BASIS OF A NEWSPAPER ARTICLE'

An anonymous samizdat communication concerning the raid by Tbilisi young communists on a Tbilisi church during Easter 1974.

This year unusual 'parishioners' visited the Easter ceremony in Tbilisi churches. These were workers of the Tbilisi committee of the Georgian Komsomol and also workers of district committees of the Komsomol. Amongst them were:

N. Lekishvili, 3rd secretary of the Tbilisi City Komsomol Committee
N. Bichiashvili, Secretary of the Kirov District Komsomol Committee
Ts. Korshiya, Secretary of the Ordzhonikidze District Committee of the Komsomol
B. Kadagidze, 2nd secretary of the Ordzhonikidze District Committee, and
O. Baratashvili head of the sport section of the Tbilisi City Komsomol Committee.

Some of the young communists were inside the churches, observing the young people. They were interested in those, especially the young communists, who go to church at Easter to pray and light a candle. To disguise themselves effectively the young communist spies lit candles themselves and pretended to pray; they clowned around and caused the believers disturbance. Such was the behaviour of, for example, the above-mentioned 3rd secretary of the Tbilisi City Komsomol Committee, N. Lekishvili. He lit a candle in Kashveti church, crossed himself and thus aroused the laughter of some girls, friends of his and young communists, who were standing nearby and also feigning prayer (most unsuccessfully, however).

Another section of the Komsomol workers stood in the street and waited for the young people, who were largely students who had 'dared' to light a candle in church. On their leaving the church,

---

[3] *Service Orthodoxe de Presse*, no. 35, February 1979; Fairy von Lilienfeld, 'Oosterse kroniek': Georgie, *Het Christelijk Oosten*, January 1980, pp. 46–52.

the young communists suggested they should accompany them to the headquarters of the people's militia which had been set up not far from the church. Near the Kashveti church of Saint George these headquarters had been set up in the manager's office of the Rustaveli cinema. Already a uniformed militia worker was sitting here, writing out the forenames and surnames of the young people who had been to church and all the information concerning them.

Near the Sion Cathedral such a headquarters was also set up in the medical centre where young people were interrogated as well. Amongst the detainees were:

V. Kurtsikidze, a student at the building faculty of the Georgian Polytechnical Institute

G. Gedevanishvili, a 3rd year student at the Tbilisi State University

E. Vasileva, a worker at the Scientific Research Institute of road construction

M. Vasileva, a worker at the knitting factory no. 2

L. Nedosekina, a student at the 65th Trade School

E. Babilov, a pupil in the 10th class of the 100th Tbilisi Secondary School

N. Malakhiyeva, a worker in a toy factory

G. Chiburdanidze, a 10th class pupil

G. Uzilashvili, a pupil in the 10th class of 13th Secondary School

S. Metreveli, a pupil of the 61st Secondary School

M. Glakhoshvili, a pupil in the 27th Secondary School

A. Mandzhavidze, a worker in the Kamo foundry

D. Davdadze, a typist of the presidium of the Georgian Academy of Sciences

T. Ochigava, a shop assistant in a book shop

N. Dugashvili, a pedagogue; his sister, D. Dugashvili, and their friends N. Zviadauri and O. Metreveli

N. Metreveli, a female student in the 2nd class of the 87th Secondary School

R. Chikviladze, a female student in the 10th class of the Oni District Secondary School

G. Tkebulava, a female student of philology in the Tbilisi State University

T. Tvaradze, a worker of the Institute of Physics and a young communist

D. Tsomaya, a former worker at the factory of volatile oils

I. Korobchinskaya, a female student at the 60th trade school

L. Pochikailo, senior inspector of the personnel department of the calculating machine factory

N. Shalitauri and V. Panfilov, young communists and workers at the philarmonia

G. Siradze, a young communist

M. Sulayeva, a young communist

M. Gabichvadze, a female student in the 20th secondary school and her friend, D. Guramishvili, and others.

In the Georgian newspaper *Tbilisi* of 15 April 1974 appeared an article entitled 'Burning Candles and Forgotten Duty'. The writer, the secretary of the Tbilisi City Committee of the Komsomol and a correspondent of the newspaper *Tbilisi*, was A. Shangelia. Almost all the above-mentioned names of detained young people figure in the given article. It says that, although the Soviet Constitution proclaims freedom of conscience, one cannot reconcile oneself to the fact that young people celebrate a religious festival, especially when they are members of the young communists. As is evident, the writers of the article intend to amend the Soviet Constitution which proclaims freedom of conscience in our country—*for all*. From their reasoning it follows that only the aged may take advantage of freedom of conscience, but young people—no.

The following fact which was not mentioned in the article is noteworthy. During the Easter ritual a young woman came out of the Sion Cathedral carrying a year-old baby. Near the headquarters of the people's militia her path was blocked by the secretary of the Ordzhonikidze District Komsomol Committee, Tsiuri Korshiya, together with other colleagues. They suggested she accompany them to the headquarters. The woman refused. Then they tore the baby from her arms and dragged her into the headquarters by force. The woman cried out. This time one of the citizens took her part and was also asked to come along to the headquarters. The citizen refused this proposal and began to accuse them of criminal action. The Komsomol workers in a powerless fury brought the child back and the woman disappeared. The citizen also continued on his way, not hearing the Komsomol leader's torrent of unprintable language.

In a private talk certain Komsomol workers acknowledged that they themselves were displeased with their own actions but had had no alternative since all this was ordered by the Party and government.

(c) ARMENIAN GREGORIAN CHURCH

The Armenian Church enjoys a degree of freedom that is greater than in any other Soviet republic. There is said to be virtually no persecution of believers of the national church.[1] Religious literature is openly on sale on parish bookstalls, post-card portraits of the Patriarch Catholicos Vazgen I are sold widely in kiosks and church music is played extensively in state concert houses and elsewhere. The price that the church pays is total commitment to Soviet rule in Armenia and the role of ambassador for the USSR to the Armenian diaspora. The Armenian Church has made the most of the opportunity afforded by the desire of the Soviet authorities to woo the Armenian community outside the Soviet Union. Many Armenians abroad believe that Soviet rule is infinitely preferable to Turkish rule. On the other hand there is a movement within Armenia for national independence, and campaigners for independence would like to see the church taking a lead and breaking out of the restrictions on political action and comment imposed by the Soviet government and accepted by the church leaders. This position is illustrated in a memorandum from Eduard Arutyunyan, leader of the Armenian Helsinki Group, arrested on 13 July 1979. He called on the Patriarch-Catholicos of the church to appeal to the Soviet government for the release of all political prisoners.

DOCUMENT 14:
PETITION TO HIS HOLINESS THE SUPREME PATRIARCH-
CATHOLICOS OF ALL ARMENIANS VAZGEN I, 18 APRIL 1976

. . .Your Holiness! Now I want to draw your attention to the decree of January 1918 [On the Separation of Church and State, Ed.]. . .

[1] See Eduard Oganessyan, 'The Armenian Church in the USSR', *Religion in Communist Lands*, vol. vii, no. 4, Winter 1979, pp. 238–42.

I shall cite some points on which this decree is violated by the Soviet government, which allows the Holy Armenian Church to ignore the section of the decree referring to a ban in involvement in the political life of the country. . .

In accordance with the 1936 Constitution priests are given electoral rights as citizens of the USSR. However, priests have only passive electoral rights, i.e. the right to vote, but not to be elected to representative public bodies, despite the fact that they represent a substantial minority of the population—the believers.

According to the decree the church exists through the gifts of believers and the state has no right to interfere in the financial activities of religious organizations. However, in practice we see that the situation is often different.

The decree separated the church from the state. This was so until 1943. It is well known that in pre-revolutionary Russia the church was under the supervision of the government through the Over-Procurator of the Holy Synod. In the USSR in 1943 a body for the supervision of the church was also created in the shape of the Council for the Affairs of the Russian Orthodox Church, and in 1944 a body for supervising the activities of sectarian groups and other religions, the Council for the Affairs of Religious Cults, was created. While the Procurator of the Synod was a single official, the Council for Religious Affairs and its officials operate in every republic of the union, and in every autonomous republic, autonomous region, national district, province and region.

. . .The Decree on the Separation of Church and State did not provide for the formation of any organizations to supervise the church. But today to talk of the separation of the state from the church is absurd.

In contradiction to the decree the state often promotes the involvement of the church in international political relations, for example in questions of the campaign for peace throughout the world, participation in the peace movement, in calling for the solution of world problems by negotiation, for disarmament and the banning of nuclear weapons. The government of the USSR, ignoring the fact that all this corresponds to the Christian commandments, interprets this as civic, not political, action on the part of the clergy. . . There is no mention of the fact that church leaders are speaking not for themselves, but for their respective churches, and that this is not civic activity but involvement in the sphere of action of the state.

Therefore I request you personally and the Echmiadzin Church

Council to approach the Soviet government, as a political act, with a petition for the release of Armenian political prisoners. . .'

III.

The Evangelical Churches

(a) EVANGELICAL CHRISTIANS AND BAPTISTS

It seems to have been part of Soviet policy towards the Protestants since 1944 to force as many streams as possible to merge with what is now called the All-Union Council of Evangelical Christians and Baptists (ECBs). Lutherans have never been pushed into such a union, however, which was instituted not primarily by the Protestants themselves for reasons of ecumenism, but by the state to facilitate its attempts at control.

Baptists—the term is normally used to signify Evangelical Christians as well—suffered as much under Khrushchev as the Orthodox did in the matter of enforced closure of churches. Possibly there was a drop of over half in the 5,400 congregations registered before 1960.[1] Since 1968 there has been scattered evidence about the re-registration of individual churches, and the process seems to have been accelerated during the 1970s.

A recent but rather special case of the total outlawing of a Protestant group is that of the Council of Churches of the Evangelical Christians and Baptists.[2] This group went into schism from the All-Union Council, not for any strictly theological or doctrinal reason, but because its members believed passionately that it was illegal for the state to interfere in church affairs. Its leaders constantly quoted the Leninist principle of the separation of church and state in support of their own position and two of them, Georgi Vins and Gennadi Kryuchkov, went on from this in a notable document[3] to claim that the 1929 Law was irreconcilable with this principle. This criticism of Soviet law, although justified and carefully presented, inevitably brought down the full wrath of the Soviet state upon the leaders of this movement.

[1] Michael Bourdeaux, *Religious Ferment in Russia*, London, 1968, p. 2.
[2] Extensive documentation on this reform movement which began in 1961 has been presented in *Religious Ferment*.
[3] *Religious Ferment*, pp. 105–13.

One of the accusations which has been constantly reiterated against these *Initsiativniki* (Action Group) Baptists, as they are commonly called in the Soviet Union, is that they 'refuse to keep the Soviet law'. Such allegations have not only been repeated incessantly in the Soviet press, but they have also been spread to foreign contacts by official representatives of the All-Union Council. In fact, these reform Baptists often know more about their legal rights than their detractors, but have rarely been able to avail themselves of them. They have, for example, consistently been unable to register their own congregations, although they have persistently sought this and are legally entitled to do so. Then the police move in to break up their meetings, claiming that they are illegal. The organizers have been heavily and repeatedly fined. In cases where officials are willing to register their churches, they usually insist on unacceptable conditions. The reform Baptists have sought to establish their right to teach religion privately to their children, and it was probably with their activities specifically in mind that one clause of the March 1966 clarification of the Penal Code made the organization of Sunday school more explicitly illegal than ever before.

Paradoxically, the Baptists are now at once among the most favoured and the most persecuted religious groups in the Soviet Union. It should not be imagined, however, that there is a clear division between the state-recognized Baptists and the others, nor that persecution is the lot exclusively of the latter. Not only are the state-recognized Baptists subjected to some types of discrimination (in university education, for example), but this can extend to non-Baptist relatives. Discrimination has often been exercised against the children of religious believers at school—where the classes include compulsory lessons in atheism throughout the Soviet Union.

Conditions for Baptists in prison have often been especially severe and there have been over 1,000 of them held at various times since 1960. Nikolai Khmara, a recent convert, was tortured to death in prison in January 1964, immediately after having been sentenced to three years for his religious activities.[4]

Georgi Vins, one of the two key leaders of the *Initsiativniki*, now exiled to the West, was treated so badly during both his periods of imprisonment (1966–9 and 1974–9) that his family and friends

---

[4] See an account in the Soviet press as well as documents from the Baptists themselves—*Religious Ferment*, pp. 77–83.

feared for his life. He attributes the fact that he was not allowed to die to Western protests which brought better treatment.

This excessively harsh treatment by the authorities is one continuing aspect of reform Baptist life. More recent deaths in prison have been Ivan Afonin (November 1969); the old man Alexei Iskovskikh (1970); in July 1971 Pavel Zakharov died as a result of his sufferings in prison; Georgi Kudryaskov died in prison in August 1972; Nikolai Melnikov died also in August as a result of prison sufferings.

In July 1972 there occurred the martyrdom of Vanya Moiseyev, a twenty-year-old soldier from Moldavia. While serving his military duty in the Crimea, he incurred the growing wrath of his superiors for his fearless Christian witness. After a number of punishments which failed to break his spirit, he was eventually tortured and drowned in the shallows of the Black Sea. The incident has attracted such lively attention in the Soviet Union and worldwide that the Soviet authorities have attempted a widespread but unconvincing cover-up. The Baptist documents on the case are remarkable for their restrained quality, and the most recent letters testify to the purifying effect the incident has had on Baptist believers and, indeed, on some atheists. The death itself has been repeatedly confirmed by the Soviet authorities, though the cause of death has been contested.[5]

Persecution of the reform Baptists continues throughout the Soviet Union. Of particular note is the church in Barnaul, where the constant harassment by the authorities has driven believers to relinquish their passports (essential identity documents) in protest at their lack of fundamental human rights.[6] The pressure on the children has also been so great that for some time Baptist parents withdrew them from the schools. The single most important item of Baptist literature is the *Bulletin of the Council of Prisoners' Relatives*. Founded in 1971, this is the organ of a Council dedicated to the gathering and dissemination of accurate and painstaking details on Baptists who have been imprisoned. The Council consists of wives and mothers of prisoners, and was first set up in 1964.

The inaugural conference, which took place in Moscow on 23 February 1964, set out the tasks and objectives of the new Council. These were first to keep church members informed about persecutions and imprisonments in all parts of the USSR so as to

[5] See *Vanya*, by Myrna Grant, Kingsway publications, 1975.
[6] See *A Song in Siberia*, by Anita and Peter Deyneka, Collins, 1978.

encourage prayer for those in need, and secondly to petition the Soviet government on behalf of the sufferers. A third task was essential to these two : that of keeping files on all prisoners and children of Christian parents taken into the care of the state.

Since 1964 a steady flow of documents has been reaching the West through the CPR. These have a distinctive manner, presenting a wealth of circumstantial detail about the oppression of believers by the Soviet government and displaying a sound knowledge of the constitutional law. The documents are marked by a complete integrity and objectivity : although they are often moving in the extreme, whether through the depth of their pathos or the demonstration of the endurance of Christian joy under duress, they can never be said to be emotionally presented. It is the stark facts themselves which impress.

Another major achievement of the CPR has been the regular production of 'prisoner lists'. These are stark documents, providing now the bare details of each prisoner's name and date of birth, date of arrest, the article of the Criminal Code under which he was condemned, the length and type of his sentence, his home address, number of dependants and the address of the prison or camp where he is held. This is the nearest thing we possess to statistics on the persecution of Baptist groups. Information contained in these lists has become more detailed over the years.

The first issue of the *Bulletin of the Council of Prisoners' Relatives*[7] appeared in April 1971 and contained the report of a conference held in Moscow by the CPR (enlarged). Since then a further sixty-six issues have been issued, all of which have reached the West. Most are of a general nature, while others concentrate on a particular individual, such as Gennadi Kryuchkov (September 1971) and Lidia Vins[8] (July 1971), the transcript of whose trial is given.

The CPR avoids dwelling too much on the negative side of the Church's life, emphasizing the flowering of faith under persecution. It discourages hatred, but seeks reconciliation based on justice, and the establishment of the Christian's right to contribute something entirely positive to the society in which he lives.

As well as turning out the *Bulletins of the Council of Prisoners' Relatives* on duplicating machines, the *Initsiativniki* have also combated the shortage of Christian literature in the USSR by the creation of clandestine printing presses. Two presses have been

[7] See Document 15, p. 55.
[8] Mrs Lidia Vins is the mother of Georgi Vins mentioned above, and she was President of the CPR from its foundation till her arrest in December 1970.

uncovered, in 1974 on a farm in Latvia and in 1977 in a house in a small town near Leningrad.[9] However, it is known that a number of presses operate simultaneously, for the discovery of both these presses was announced on a printed leaflet. The presses have concentrated on spiritual literature, rather than protests, and have produced New Testaments, regular journals, and most recently whole Bibles, as well as reprinting Christian books translated into Russian. So extensive has the printing work been that there have been sufficient New Testaments to supply registered churches. The embarrassment caused by this has led to the printing or import of Bibles, hymnbooks and concordances by the registered All-Union Council of ECBs, totalling 150,000 items in the period 1974–9.

The attractiveness of the unregistered churches for young people especially has caused the authorities to permit the registered churches to conduct youth work, although this is still technically illegal. Although reconciliation between the *Initsiativniki* and the registered leadership appears remote, the unregistered movement has served to bring about many other changes in the registered churches, including an unexpected degree of democratic control and accountability of church leaders to the membership. This will inevitably lead to tensions as leaders are forced to admit that they are restricted in what they can achieve by the secular authorities.

DOCUMENT 15:
APPEAL FROM THE COUNCIL OF ECB PRISONERS' RELATIVES

To: the Presidium of the USSR Supreme Soviet, the Politburo of the Central Committee of the CPSU.
Copies to: the USSR Procuracy, the USSR Committee of State Security (KGB), the Permanent Soviet Representative at the UNO
To all Christians of the world, all heads of governments in the world, to the Council of ECB Churches in the USSR.

From the Council of ECB Prisoners' Relatives, those suffering for the Word of God in the USSR.

'And the Lord said: Because the cry of Sodom and Gomorrah is great, and because their sin is very grievous, I will go down now and see whether they have done altogether according to the cry of

---

[9] A third printing press was discovered in a suburb of Dnepropetrovsk on 19 January 1980.

it, which is come unto me; and if not, I will know.' (Gen. 18: 20–21)

January 1978. We have entered a New Year once more. Our whole planet Earth has passed through yet another stage—the last year—in its headlong flight towards eternity.

At the beginning of 1976, we wrote you a detailed New Year letter about the true position of the believers living within the territory of the USSR. That letter covered an extensive period of time, including details of the past.

At the beginning of 1977, we again sent you a New Year letter. Your silent answer was expressed in the cruel actions against Christians which followed, actions which filled to the brim the cup of our suffering for the right to believe and to worship the true living God, Creator of heaven and earth. After such actions, it became clear that our letters to you were completely useless.

Later, paying no attention to the tears of suffering Christians and the cries of children, you did not put an end to your cruel deeds against the believers, but intensified them in accordance with the New Constitution, and after its adoption embarked on a course which aimed at the complete extermination of religious believers.

With such cunning aims, you deliberately refused to take into account any suggestions put forward by believers concerning the draft Constitution, so that they would have some defence, be given some rights in the country and be able to serve God sincerely, fulfilling all the commands of Jesus Christ. You did not publish a single suggestion in defence of their rights. The Council of ECB Prisoners' Relatives warned you, even before the Constitution was adopted, that if it was adopted in the draft text, legal extermination would be the fate of Christians. However, you paid no attention to that either.

Not a single amendment averting the situation threatening true Christians was made to any article of the Constitution which concerned the civil rights of believers.

The new Constitution has been adopted. Now you have established and legalized your right physically to exterminate the believers. Thus our declaration was confirmed in real life immediately after the adoption of the Constitution.

In various parts of the country new repressions against the believers flared up with fresh violence. Prayer meetings were cruelly broken up (in the towns of Bryansk, Gorlovka in Donetsk region, Rostov, Magnitogorsk and others).

Searches in the flats of believers, which would be better called robberies, often involving direct attempts to steal the private property of the believers, were renewed at the same time throughout the country.

The greediness of the officials who carried out the searches at the homes of believers often surpassed anything that had occurred before.

As a result of these latest searches a great deal of religious literature was confiscated. Ten thousand books were confiscated in the town of Dzhetysai, in Central Asia, alone. In the town of Semipalatinsk a great deal of spiritually instructive literature was also confiscated. We draw your attention to the fact that literature is being confiscated in single copies from individual believers, during the dispersal of prayer meetings, while boarding aeroplanes and in other situations. This has already become an ordinary fact of life for believing Christians in this country.

In the town of Dzhambul, about 22,000 roubles of church funds were confiscated during searches. Is this not stealing from several hundred believers who made their individual contributions to the good of the Church in the name of the Lord?

Searches were carried out in the towns of Dzhambul, Dzhetysai, Alma-Ata, Rostov, Kiev, in Donetsk region, Bryansk, Kharkov and Leningrad. An illegal search, infringing a number of laws, was carried out in Kiev in the flat of Lydia Mikhailovna Vins, a member of the Council of ECB Prisoners' Relatives, and religious literature was confiscated without record.

Pastors of the ECB Church and ordinary Christians are being arrested again on various pretexts in an intensified new wave of pressure.

Grigory Vasilievich Kostyuchenko, pastor of the ECB Church in Timoshevsk, Krasnodar territory, has been arrested and sentenced to one year's imprisonment for parasitism.

On what basis by such arrests are you depriving the Church of the right to choose its own pastors as it thinks fit, and to release them from factory work? The Church has every right to do so, in obedience both to the Lord and according to the law. However, the various reservations and omissions in the Constitution have given full rein to those who have been longing to wipe out even the mention of believers and of the Lord's name in our land.

Ivan Yakovlevich Antonov, pastor of the Church in Kirovograd and member of the Council of Churches, has been arrested on the same kind of pretext.

Pyotr Danilovich Peters, pastor of the Church in Rostov and evangelist of the Council of Churches, has also been arrested.

In addition, criminal charges have been brought against the following pastors of the ECB Church: Yakov Grigorevich Skornyakov (Dzhambul), Pavel Timofeevich Rytikov (Krasnodon, Voroshilovgrad region), Yevgeny Nikiforovich Pushkov (Khartsyzsk, Donetsk region), Nikolai Georgievich Baturin, member of the Council of Churches (Shakhty, Rostov region); while Dmitry Vasilevich Minyakov (Valga) and Mikhail Ivanovich Khorev (Kishinev), members of the ECB Council of Churches, have been detained more than once by state officials.

On what basis do you constantly interfere in the Church's affairs in this way and prevent its pastors from serving the Lord in their churches?

And all this is fully approved and legalized against the background of the new Constitution.

A constant search is going on for the President of the Council of Churches, Gennady Konstantinovich Kryuchkov, so that he can be arrested.

For many years now, since her youth, the Christian Aida Skripnikova (Leningrad) has been persecuted: she has already served two terms of imprisonment and has been deprived of a residence permit in Leningrad by the Leningrad authorities; the new Constitution reinforces and gives fresh support to these actions by the authorities.

A case is being fabricated against Fyodor Vladimirovich Makhovitsky, presbyter of the Leningrad ECB Church, with the aim of arresting him.

The new Constitution has granted the right to arrest and bring criminal charges against ECB believers, often leaving out any charge of infringing the legislation on religious cults and accusing believers of crimes contradicting Christian teaching.

Thus a criminal case was brought against Anatoly Alexandrovich Petrenko, pastor of the ECB Church in Shostky, Sumy region. There was an attempt to charge him with stealing state property and speculation.

These charges were based on anonymous letters and photographs of various everyday objects such as clothes (old and new) and sheets (new and old, even some put out for washing), which were taken during a search of Petrenko's flat.

In Omsk region, in the village of Novo-Alexandrovka, Moskalensk district, brothers K. K. Gur and A. A. Penner (a 73-year-old man) have been arrested on an obviously falsified charge of beating up a teenage girl. This unheard-of lie is being upheld by the representatives of authority.

In addition, everywhere young Christian men, who have been called up into the Soviet army and have refused to take the military oath, are being threatened with prosecution; criminal cases are being made out against them and many have already been sentenced to various terms of imprisonment. These innocent boys, children still, are being thrown into the dreadful conditions of camp life, where debauchery flourishes, that awful foul-mouthed world where horrifying crimes are an ordinary fact of life. Many of them have fathers who also spent time in the camps for their Christian views, and who know quite well what it means for Christian boys to find themselves in that criminal, debauched camp world, and how the conditions of camp life can shake the spirit.

We receive letters from all over the country—cries from the hearts of mothers who have seen their innocent sons off into the army to be threatened with prosecution for refusing to take the military oath.

We have already explained to you more than once the reason for this behaviour on the part of young Christians. It is a direct command of Jesus Christ: 'Swear not at all'. How can we and our children break Christ's commandment?

If you are not willing to agree that the sons of Christians will not be forced to take the military oath or prosecuted for this, then Christian mothers are ready to appeal to world public opinion and declare that they do not bring their sons into the world and nurture them so that their youth can be destroyed in the conditions of criminal camp life.

Christians do not refuse to serve in the ranks of the army. Young Christians do their military service conscientiously. In private conversations with officers of the military units, parents of Christian sons serving in the army hear good reports of them as the most disciplined, well brought up, dependable and honest soldiers.

However, more than ten young Christians have already been sentenced for refusing to take the military oath. Many have been threatened with prosecution and criminal cases have been made out against them.

For example, a criminal case has been made out against Ivan Grigorevich Rotar, now on military service in the settlement of Arkhara, v/ch [*voennaya chast* = unit] 74571 'A', in the Amur region. A criminal case has also been brought against Vladimir

Mikhailovich Zhikhor, now serving in the settlement of Solne-
chny, v/ch 45783, Khabarovsk territory; Alexandr Mikhailovich
Pugachov, in v/ch 29681, Rostov Veliky, Yaroslavl region, is
being threatened with prosecution for refusing to take the oath,
and so on.

Young Nikolai Kravchenko, beaten and maimed while in the
army, was discharged after unsuccessful treatment of his broken
jaw. In the town of Sumy, where Kravchenko lives, doctors have
refused to accept that he is ill or to give him a medical exemption,
thus forcing him to go out to work. He is in bad health and is in
constant danger of paralysis.

Christian prisoners are condemned to long terms in camps and
exile. From the south, they are to serve these terms in the far
north, in the wilds, with the aim of physically exterminating them.

That was what happened to G. P. Vins, Secretary of the ECB
Council of Churches, a resident of Ukraine, who was sent to serve
his term of imprisonment in the wilds of cold Yakutia. His health
has been undermined and his life is in constant danger. A medical
commission, set up because of the insistence of believers, specially
and deliberately declared him healthy. G. P. Vins is still confined
and suffering in a Yakutian camp.

A native of southern Ukraine, Stepan Grigorievich Germanyuk
from Voroshilovgrad region, has been exiled—quite clearly with
the deliberate aim of killing him—to the settlement of Chumikan,
Khabarovsk territory, on the shores of the Sea of Okhotsk. The
climate is unbelievably severe: frosts of 50–60°C; bleak, cold storm
winds from the sea, and the low air pressure and lack of oxygen
constantly put his health and life at risk. According to the reckon-
ing of the local inhabitants, only about 20 per cent of people sent
there survive. The rest perish, either because of the climatic conditions or at the hands of the local inhabitants. Stepan
Grigorievich's health has already been undermined by four years'
imprisonment in camps.

This never-ending stream of events, spreading like lightning
throughout the land and seen in the increased repression of believers everywhere, is nothing less than a centralized decision, backed
by the Constitution, to wipe out any attempt to confess the Lord's
name in the USSR.

We insist on the immediate release of the Christians already
arrested, the immediate review of cases of Christians condemned
and their release. We insist that you should not interfere in the

Church's affairs or in its services. Give the pastors of the Church the opportunity to hold services freely.

Put an end to your intended extermination of Christians and their mass arrests.

You may exterminate us, but the whole world is watching us and can see it.

And we, as relatives of the prisoners, as relatives of Christians inevitably threatened by extermination for faith in the Lord and loyalty to him, must call on you to stop this, put an end to it! Do not think that the Lord is slow in coming to the aid of his chosen. He is not slow, but long-suffering towards you.

Know that the Lord will soon help his chosen. We do not say this ourselves: so speaks the Word of God which cannot be refuted. And the Word of God will not pass away, for it is written, 'Heaven and earth will pass away, but My words will not pass away.'

So hold your trials and do justice!

Reply to the address:
Voroshilovgrad region
Krasnodon 1, Podgornaya 30
Rytikova, Galina Yurievna

The Council of ECB Prisoners' Relatives, those condemned for the Word of God in the USSR.

Signed:

1. *A. Melashchenko* (Seversk, Donetsk region)
2. *A. A. Senkevich* (Grodno)
3. *V. P. Dombrovskaya* (Saki, Crimean region)
4. *L. M. Vins* (Kiev)
5. *A. T. Kozorezova* (Voroshilovgrad)
6. *L. V. Rumachik* (Dedovsk, Moscow region)
7. *S. A. Yudintseva* (Khartsyzsk, Donetsk region)
8. *Z. Ya. Velchinskaya* (Brest)

(b) PENTECOSTALS

The number of Soviet Pentecostals can only be guessed. According to official Evangelical Christian-Baptist records 33,000 of them belong to the Evangelical Christian-Baptist Union, while a further 20,000 worship independently. Unofficially they estimate 100–150,000 adult baptized members, and this figure corresponds to a well-informed Soviet scholar's estimate of one quarter or one fifth of the numbers of Evangelical Christians and Baptists, whose membership stands at 550,000. If one adds non-baptized adult adherents and dependent children a figure of 400–500,000 Pentecostals, as suggested by recent western press reports, is not unlikely.

Of this number a small proportion have expressed the desire to emigrate from the USSR, about 30,000 persons, including children. Many others may wish to emigrate, but have not yet been able to make their wishes known outside the USSR. However, a large number, almost certainly the great majority, wish to remain in the USSR and desire an improvement in their position.

About 550 congregations or groups belong to the Evangelical Christian-Baptist Union on the basis of an agreement reached in 1945 (the August Agreement), which is generally believed to have been brought about by pressure from the Soviet government. Many of the Pentecostals who united with the Evangelical Christians and Baptists, including one of the four representatives who signed the August Agreement, subsequently, within about two years, became disillusioned with it and opted for an independent and illegal existence. The Evangelical Christian-Baptist Union has over 500 such groups recorded on its files, but the number is almost certainly considerably more. The main point of contention is speaking in tongues (glossalalia) which Pentecostals believe to be a sign of the Baptism in the Holy Spirit. In the August Agreement they bound themselves not to use tongues in public worship and not to spread the doctrine of the Baptism in the Holy Spirit accompanied by tongues among other members of united congregations. The Evangelical Christians and Baptists agreed not to attack this doctrine and not to discriminate against Pentecostals in making church appointments. Both sides have failed to keep these undertakings, which has caused much friction and not infrequent schisms. Many Pentecostals remaining in united congregations are unhappy about their position. The situation is rather better where congregations belonging to the Union are in fact wholly Pentecostal in membership. The reason for the continuation of this uneasy union has been the refusal of the authorities to grant recognition to Pentecostals as a separate denomination. Any activity outside the Union has been illegal and subject to repressive measures.

Recently, however, this position has changed in that the authorities are now prepared to register autonomous Pentecostal congregations, though an independent Pentecostal Union, which has been demanded since 1947, has not yet been allowed. However, the conditions attached to registration are unacceptable to most Pentecostals and so far only about ninety congregations have accepted autonomous registration. Many of these seem to have been formed by Pentecostals who formerly belonged to registered Evangelical Christian-Baptist churches, for whom autonomous registration means an improvement in conditions. Especially since the signing of the Helsinki Agreements considerable pressure has been brought to bear on some congregations in an attempt to force them to register. For example in Berdichev (Zhitomir region, Ukraine) the presbyter and the deacon have been threatened with arrest if the congregation does not register. In the city of Zhitomir pressure to register began early in 1976. The criminal file on the presbyter S. Demyanchuk was reopened, although he had already been convicted, imprisoned and amnestied for war crimes. The congregation was given three months in which to make up its mind whether to register. In Zhitintsy (Zhitomir region) the Pentecostal congregation was allowed to meet freely after the signing of the Helsinki Agreements. However, when the congregation refused to register the authorities resumed fining the members for organizing services. In Chernovtsy (Western Ukraine) the presbyter was arrested and sentenced to five years detention when he refused to agree to registration. Then the congregation was registered. Such registration is enforced rather than voluntary. Pentecostals believe this is being done in order to give an impression of greater religious freedom by having Pentecostal show churches for visitors. For this reason great efforts have been made to get the Moscow Pentecostals to register; and a small group agreed to register in 1979.

Even when offered registration without conditions most refuse, for they know of congregations where the authorities subsequently attempt to enforce the conditions by threats to withdraw registration. The conditions rejected include a ban on organized charitable activity, a ban on organized religious education for the children and on their attendance at church or participation in services (the application of the ruling on children seems to vary from place to place), a requirement to report any visitors from other congregations to the authorities and not to allow them to preach and the submission of all office-bearers to the local authorities for vetting. They normally exclude all ex-prisoners. Since the Pentecostal movement has been illegal for fifty years most of the experienced leaders have been imprisoned for their religious activities at one time or another.

Pentecostals regard these conditions as unconstitutional interference in church affairs and unacceptable limitations on their freedom. They prefer the freedom of illegality, organizing themselves and worshipping 'in accordance with the dictates of their own conscience', even at the price of limitation of services, fines and arrests.

DOCUMENT 16:
THE SPIRIT OF HELSINKI AND THE SPIRIT OF ATHEISM

A year has gone by since the moment when the 'Final Act' of the Conference on Security and Cooperation in Europe was signed at Helsinki. When this document was published, many short-sighted religious believers were glad: 'At last!' they thought. 'Now we shall no longer be fined, tried and libelled in the press!' (a pleasant error). After all, the countries which signed—including ours—had promised to 'recognize and respect the freedom of the individual to express his religion or faith, alone or together with others, and to act in accordance with his own conscience'.

'In accordance with his own conscience'—well said! Perhaps a time of peace—even the thousand-year reign of peace—had begun? When Mikhail Shokhov, one of the Pentecostal Christian presbyters of Moscow, read this out to the group he was leading, saying that a time of real freedom had begun, he was summoned by the

KGB and told that he had misunderstood what had been published: there would be no changes in our country with regard to believers, that it was too soon to shout 'hurrah!', that the believers would have to shout 'help!' instead. However, the atheists are far-sighted: they have a great deal of experience behind them already. You can't shout 'help!' if you've been gagged. For example, the believers of Donetsk region were fined, but they were then summoned and deprived of the receipts for the fines they had paid, in case these might end up in the West. And so you can't shout for help.

The Pentecostal Christians, constantly referred to as a forbidden, fanatical sect, are being offered forcible registration, while the Baptists of Sverdlovsk region—who have asked for registration— are being denied it (and these are not Baptists who support the Council of Churches, but those belonging to the All-Union ECB Council!) There is no paradox in this, merely a difference in the methods of struggle between the stick and the carrot, as one of our theologians has said.

In Zhitomir region, where the atheists are really working hard for their daily bread, the local authorities (mostly in the villages)— after reading the Helsinki declaration—told the believers that they would now be free, that no one would break up their meetings, or fine them. Alas they spoke too soon. After things had been 'explained' to them by the district *soviet* executive committees, the village authorities said they had been too hasty, that nothing had changed.

The same anti-religious campaign is going on in the press. The newspaper *Vinnitskaya Pravda*, for example, in an article on 10 July 1976, 'They can't hide behind their shadows' by G. Osipov and V. Gaichenko, writes that Pentecostals Vasily Matyash and Vasily Romanyuk fought against Soviet power during the war, with a prayer book in one hand and a rifle in the other—although it was not like that at all. They were not believers during the war, but came to believe in the camps where they were serving sentences for their past deeds. The authors make mention of Pavel Kuzmich, who became rich—or so they write—by working together with his wife (not, of course, without the knowledge of the administrative authorities).

We have already written that *Vinnitskaya Pravda* often prints libels under the title of 'Atheism—forward to the attack!', speaking of the past as if it were the present, stating that a believer did something when this either happened before he became a believer, or never occurred at all.

The paper calls on communists and atheists to fight constantly against sectarian 'teachings' and to show up the Pentecostals for what they really are.

On the anniversary of the historic agreement, when our press writes a great deal about the spirit of Helsinki, the spirit of atheism has shown its refusal to compromise: believers from the settlements of Malakhovka and Tomilino near Moscow were surrounded during a service in the woods by policemen, volunteer militia and persons in civilian clothes; they had their names taken: the preachers had their Bibles confiscated and were later fined. Among these believers, there were people who had rejoiced that they would no longer be persecuted or fined, as in past years, that they would be able to express their faith 'in accordance with their own consciences'.

Denis Karpenko
August 1976.

DOCUMENT 17:
APPEAL TO THE WORLD COUNCIL OF CHURCHES FROM
CHRISTIANS OF THE EVANGELICAL FAITH (PENTECOSTALS)
RESIDENT IN THE USSR

[. . .]
May God make you willing to listen to us who cry to him and to you from a land of slavery and repression. We know that your sessions are attended by delegates from the USSR sent by the Moscow Patriarchate and the AUCECB [All-Union Council of Evangelical Christians and Baptists]. We do not know these people, but they do not represent those innocent Christians who are assaulted or sentenced to prison. We too would like to attend your meetings in the persons of our elected delegates, but the atheistic authorities will never allow this. Instead, they confine us within the barbed barricades of the Soviet frontiers. However, it is not the chief of our troubles that we cannot travel abroad freely like all the citizens of your free countries can whenever they wish. Our great trouble is that we are not allowed to live in peace behind the iron curtain. The Soviet Union is for us a vast concentration camp. Here we are prosecuted because we are believers and because we bring up our children in the faith. This is what is happening now. When Stalin was alive believers of all persuasions and unorthodox thinkers were condemned for nothing less than treason: some were shot, others shut up in prisons and labour camps, from

which most never returned to their homes. From those who happened to escape we know how cruel was the lot of those who lived only two or three decades ago. They were our fathers, grandfathers, brothers.

In our day things have changed a little: we are assaulted less often, sentenced less severely, but after periods in prison or labour camp we are scarcely alive and, through broken health, hardly fit to earn a living for our large families. In addition, because we will not recant our beliefs, but continue to bring up our children in the faith, we are threatened with further terms of imprisonment, and even old men are re-sentenced regardless of their age. And at the same time, there in Nairobi, you see before you those who assure you and all the world that they do not persecute believers in our country, but only criminals, and that there is no discrimination. Perhaps it is true that there is no discrimination, for there is another word for this crime against humanity, not discrimination, but genocide. Yes, it is precisely that, since we live in circumstances deliberately designed so that Christians should be remorselessly wiped off the face of the entire USSR. This is how the priests of communism want to bring about their victory.

In the 1960s we were condemned because we pressed for registration for our Christian congregations. They told us that our sect was fanatical and therefore could not be registered. They made up black slander and lies about so-called human sacrifices, and inflamed the ignorant population of towns and villages against us. Now they condemn us because we do not want to register our churches, as to Christians the conditions are unacceptable.

Oh no, we would not oppose a governmental registration such as that which exists in your countries. But you would not accept our laws on registration either were such a great tide of atheism to rise in your countries as it has here.

[. . .]

We request you, as representatives of the churches of the world, as our brothers in the faith, when you have understood the import of what we have written (and we enclose details of repressions and discrimination against us), make representations to the Soviet government to let us leave the country.

[. . .]

September 1976

(c)   SEVENTH-DAY ADVENTISTS

The brunt of persecution against Adventists in the USSR has been borne by the All-Union Church of Free and True Seventh-Day Adventists, a small but highly active denomination, which has shown remarkable tenacity in the face of atheistic communism. It is an offspring of the officially registered Seventh-Day Adventists but is not recognized by the Soviet authorities. Despite this fact, which forces it to carry on its activities clandestinely, its theology and inner workings are better known to the West than those of the registered Adventists through detailed *samizdat* which it has managed to publish and get out of the country recently in comparatively large quantities. The late leader of the 'True Remnant', as the movement calls itself, was V. A. Shelkov, a prolific writer who had spent twenty-three years in prison and was sentenced again in March of 1979 to five years strict labour in a camp for his religious activities. A dominant feature of Shelkov's and of all Adventist literature is its staunch stand against state interference in religious affairs and matters of personal conscience. This stance was the main issue which split the Adventists in 1924 and has been a wedge between them ever since.

From the beginning of Soviet rule Seventh-Day Adventists were bound to clash with the new atheistic authorities over several vital points of their doctrine. They believe that the Bible is the only directive from God for the understanding of truth in life, and place great emphasis on the second coming of Christ, hence their name Adventists, and the Ten Commandments, particularly the fourth and the sixth concerning the observance of the Sabbath and the killing of a fellow man.

It was these latter issues which caused tension between the Adventists and the Soviet government, along with their apocalyptic behaviour which accompanied their eager expectations of the second coming of Christ and interfered at times with their earthly communistic labour. In 1957 a group of peasants from the official

68

body of the Seventh-Day Adventists in Ukraine dressed in white shirts and laid on tables expecting the 'end of the world' at the bidding of the local Adventist leader. This and similar incidents made a negative impression on the Soviet authorities. The Adventist custom of observing the Sabbath as the Jews do on Saturday conflicts directly with the Soviet practice of considering Saturday a working and a school day. Adventists have continually been badgered by Soviet authorities for refusing to work on Saturdays and to send their children to school. In addition to this strict and fundamental interpretation of the sixth commandment, 'Thou shalt not kill', has lead to a pacifistic streak in the Adventist faith. Since Soviet law demands that all young men at eighteen enter the military for two years service, this Adventist tendency to pacificism has drawn the disapproval of Soviet officials. This became quite a grave matter during the Second World War when refusal to serve by Adventists (many of whom were of German extraction) was construed as treason and was harshly punished. In 1960 Soviet authorities, during the Krushchev crackdown on religion, charged the official wing of Seventh-Day Adventists with embezzling and deprived them of their Union. Today they exist in independent registered congregations but without an organizing Union such as that which the Evangelical Christians and Baptists have.

After the 1924 split the principle of separation of church and state became a prominent mark of the True Remnant. The subject was and is much discussed in their writings. They are particularly critical of what they have dubbed *gosateizm* or 'state atheism'. *Gosateizm* is direct interference by the state in religious matters by means of mandatory registration of congregations and members, restrictions on religious education, curbs on missionary activity and deprivation of the right to live by their convictions by forcing them to work and study on the Sabbath and do military service. One piece of their *samizdat* expresses their stance so:

> We recognize human authority as God given and we teach obedience to it as a holy duty as long as it functions within its own justified limits. However if its demands contradict God's demands then we are prepared to be obedient more to God than to man. We condemn and are decided opponents of any kind of intrusion and interference whatsoever by the government in

the realm of religious convictions, life and activities with the aim of regulating them.[1]

The passage from Matthew 22:21, 'Render unto Caesar that which is Caesar's and unto God that which is God's', is often quoted by Adventists as a defence of their conviction regarding church and state relationships.

The True Remnant's struggle against *gosateizm* and their determination to practise their faith despite its contradictions to Soviet ideology have earned it much suffering. The life of the late Chairman Vladimir Andrevich Shelkov reads like the record of a perpetual prisoner and fugitive. In 1927 Shelkov first started serving the Church as a preacher and was arrested shortly thereafter in 1931. After three years exile he spent the next eleven years on the run living in as many as twelve places to avoid the authorities. In 1945 he was arrested a second time and was sentenced to death. His sentence was commuted to ten years imprisonment. From 1954 to 1957 he was free until he was arrested in 1957 for the third time and again sentenced to ten years. In 1967 he returned to his family in Samarkand but lived a far from peaceful life. He was harassed, searched and arrested once though nothing came of this arrest. In March 1978 he was arrested for the fifth time at the age of eighty-two for 'infringement of persons and rights of citizens under the appearance of performing religious ceremonies' and 'the circulation of deliberately false fabrications which defame the Soviet State and social system' (arts. 147–1 and 191–4 of the Criminal Code of the Uzbek SSR). On 29 March 1979 Shelkov was sentenced to five years of strict regime camp with confiscation of property. He died in camp in Siberia on 27 January 1980, aged 84.

DOCUMENT 18:
THE ALL-UNION CHURCH OF TRUE AND FREE SEVENTH-DAY ADVENTISTS ANNOUNCES THE FORMATION OF THE GROUP TO CAMPAIGN FOR JUSTICE AND INVESTIGATE FACTS OF PERSECUTION OF BELIEVERS IN THE USSR

Given the continually increasing repression, persecution and harassment of every kind: the unremitting observation and surveillance of believers and their homes using modern audio and visual bugging devices, the interception of private correspondence and

[1] R. N. Galetsky, *Report on the Situation of Religion and Believers in the USSR*, p. 17; 'Adventist "samizdat" '.

telephone-tapping, the imposition of penalties, punishments and fines, searches involving the confiscation and theft of goods and possessions, purely religious and other literature, and personal items, the illegal and groundless arrests, trials, assaults, the use of torture and inquisitorial 'experimental' methods of interrogation to obtain the desired information, the use of special psychiatric clinics to suppress religious freedom and independence, discrimination in education, work and other areas of social life, the withdrawal of parental rights from parents who give their children a religious upbringing, and the forcible removal of children from their parents by court order to place them in special state boarding schools for enforced, atheistic re-education, the dispersal by force of unregistered religious gatherings and services, the recruitment and placing of agents among free believers, and many other tactics employed by the atheistic state dictatorship to destroy religious freedom and independent believers in the USSR;

In order to conduct an ideological campaign for justice against the atheistic state dictatorship and to expose the facts concerning persecution of believers in our country, we, the All-Union Church of True and Free Seventh-Day Adventists announce the formation of the 'Group of the All-Union Church of True and Free Seventh-day Adventists to Campaign for Justice and Investigate Facts of Persecution of Believers in the USSR.'

The aims of the group will be as follows:

to collect information and complaints from believers who belong to the All-Union Church of True and Free Seventh-Day Adventists and to other religions who are persecuted and oppressed purely for their religious beliefs, life-style and activity;

to investigate the facts concerning the use of force and tyranny by the atheistic state dictatorship;

to publicize the facts concerning the use of force and tyranny to violate all the basic rights and freedoms of independent believers. To unmask and expose the true face of state atheism before the world;

to present complaints and protests both to the local authorities in our own country and to international legal organizations dealing with human rights, and to approach the governments of those states who signed the Helsinki Agreement on co-operation and security in Europe;

to collect facts and documentary evidence on the suppression of the rights and freedoms of independent believers by the atheistic state dictatorship and the violation of the Helsinki Agreement for the coming meeting in Madrid;

to undertake legal and educational work among believing citizens who are persecuted for acknowledging religious adherence in order to expose laws that lead to confrontation and secret instructions and regulations which contravene both legitimate, internal civil laws and international laws, and are used by the atheistic state to suppress genuine religious freedom;

to render all kinds of assistance to persecuted believers and their families, who have become victims of the dictatorship of state atheism.

The group will refrain from any activity subversive to the state and aimed at undermining its purely civil authority. Civil authority is recognized by us as authorized by God, and does not infringe upon or interfere with matters of conscience, conviction, life-style and activity of independent believing citizens.

The principal aim of the group is to expose and conduct an ideological campaign against the criminal and despotic religion of evolutionary-materialistic atheism and its illegal, criminal and corrupt association with the state, that is, fornication with the kings and merchants of the earth (Rev. 17:2; 18:3).

Since any civil rights movement in the USSR meets with persecution and state vindictiveness, as is shown by past and present events, we, the All-Union Church of True and Free Seventh-Day Adventists, an organized, Christian civil rights group, appeal to all the legal organizations of the world, the heads of just states and to the international community to support our extremely difficult but just and noble fight, prophetically foretold by God, for religious and personal freedom.

The present membership of the group includes:

Group Leader *Rostislav Galetsky*
Secretary *Leonid Samoilov*
Members 1. *Nina Kuznetsova*
2. *Lyubov Sitnikova*
3. *Lyudmila Strelnikova*
4. *Nadezhda Prisypko*
5. *Anna Zubareva*
All-Union Church of True and Free
Seventh-Day Adventists

IV.

Catholics

(a) ROMAN CATHOLICS

Roman Catholics are persecuted in the Soviet Union today not only for their religious steadfastness, but for their international connections and because, to some extent, they are identified by the authorities with 'separatist' elements among Ukrainians, Belorussians, Latvians and above all Lithuanians, who make up the main body of professing Catholics in the USSR.

Since the time of Stalin, this Church has never been able to restore any central leadership. Ironically, the Russian Orthodox Church is today represented in Rome, but not the Soviet Catholics, though since the Second Vatican Council some bishops have been able to visit Rome. The only functioning dioceses today are in Latvia and Lithuania, while the difficulties in remoter areas are more acute. There are probably over three million Roman Catholics in the Soviet Union today. Here we devote special attention to Lithuania, where the greatest concentration of them resides.

When Stalin annexed Lithuania shortly before Hitler invaded it, he took over a strong and impressively-organized Church. But now the picture is very different. Monasticism, once flourishing in over a hundred centres, has been abolished. Religious journals are no more. A prayer book has been printed in an inadequate edition since the Soviet annexation. At the end of 1972, a state printing house in Vilnius, the capital of Lithuania, published the New Testament in a new Lithuanian translation and in an edition of 10,000. This in itself was wholly inadequate for the needs of the believers; in fact, distribution to the churches was desultory. Some copies went abroad, others to Communist Party workers. This still leaves one significant omission: the catechism. The one formerly in use is now unsuited to popular needs, but no permission has been forthcoming for a new one.[1]

Almost half of the churches have been closed. The number of

[1] These details are contained in *Chronicle of the Lithuanian Catholic Church*, No. 6.

priests has fallen from 1,480 in 1940 to 711 in 1979, and is still dropping. Of four seminaries, only the one at Kaunas remains. It was restricted to a maximum of 30 seminarians, so there are no more than five or six ordinations a year, while two or three times that number of priests die. However, in 1976 the numbers rose to 51.

The Roman Catholics received fewer concessions than some other religious groups during 1954–7, while 1960–64 was a period of renewed physical persecution. Quite apart from slanderous attacks against individual priest and bishops in the press, as with the Orthodox Church, travel restrictions were placed on the clergy even within their own dioceses, which prevented them from holding confirmations and dispensing the sacraments. People known to attend church or who had their children baptized found that discriminatory measures were taken against them.

The Communist Party set up a special committee in Vilnius in 1963 with the task of devising new secular 'rites' to replace traditional ones, but this campaign seems to have had even less success in Lithuania than in other parts of the Soviet Union.

Soon after the worst of the Khrushchev anti-religious crisis had passed, a very few concessions were made to the Lithuanian Catholics. The most important of these was the ordination of two bishops and two assistant bishops to three central dioceses in 1968–9. However, two bishops consecrated in the 1950s—Bishop J. Steponavičius of Vilnius (the archdiocese) and Bishop V. Sladkevičius of Kaišiadorys—have been exiled to small villages and are not allowed to carry out their episcopal duties, since the 1960s. Bishop Steponavičius was apparently too zealous in defending the rights of Catholics in his diocese, while Bishop Sladkevičius was consecrated 'without government permission'. It is rumoured that Bishop Steponavičius is the 'secret' cardinal created by Pope John Paul II.

At present there are only two active bishops—Bishop L. Povilonis of Kaunas and Vilkaviškis and Bishop R. Krikščiunas of Panevežys. Since the death of Bishop Matulaitis-Labukas in 1979, three out of six dioceses are being run by administrators.

The position of Lithuanian Catholics is an extremely difficult one. However, the most significant feature of the last decade is that they, like the Orthodox, the Baptists and the Jews, have found a voice, and a voice that has turned out to be significantly stronger. No other religious group in the USSR has been able to attract such open support from its adherents as the Lithuanian Catholic Church showed in the 1970s. There were protests about restrictions on theological education, about the difficulty of preparing children for confirmation and general discrimination against believers. Transcripts have been made of the trials of Catholic priests and somehow sent out of the country.

In 1972 a journal called the *Chronicle of the Lithuanian Catholic Church*, made its appearance. Forty numbers, the first dated 1972 and the last dealing with events up until late 1979 have now reached the West. The first number of the new *Chronicle* concentrated on the trials of Fr Juozas Zdebskis and Fr Prosperas Bubnys, sentenced in October 1971 to one year's imprisonment for catechizing children. Issue no. 2 began with a detailed account of the 'Memorandum of Lithuanian Catholics'. Written against the background of nationalist outbursts that hit world headlines in the spring of 1972, these first two issues of the Lithuanian Catholic Chronicle show a clear sequence of events as they affected the Church.

Fr Zdebskis was arrested in August 1971, charged with gathering children for religious instruction (illegal under Soviet law). His trial was prepared in secret, but on 11 October the news leaked out that it was to be held the next day in Kaunas. Thousands came to the courtroom, but were forcibly prevented from entering. In his final statement, Fr Zdebskis declared: 'I am being tried for fulfilling my rightful duties. . . If the courts do not judge us priests now, then our nation will judge us! And finally will come the hour for the true judgement by the Supreme Being. May God help us priests to fear this more than your judgement.'

Fr Bubnys at his trial (held on the same day in Raseinai) made a no less spirited defence. With the memory of these trials fresh in their mind, a group of Lithuanian believers set about organizing the 'Memorandum of Lithuanian Catholics' dated December 1971. It was addressed to Mr Brezhnev and appealed again for religious liberty. Signatures were canvassed throughout the entire republic. Only a few were afraid to sign, the *Chronicle* tells us; most added their names willingly. The final total was 17,054—there would have been many more, but for KGB interference, says an Addendum to the Memorandum.

Its organizers had learned from experience that petitions to the Kremlin never reached their destination, but ended only on the desk of J. Rugienis, the Lithuanian representative of the government Council for Religious Affairs. So they added a covering letter dated February 1972 and sent it to Dr Kurt Waldheim, General

Secretary of the United Nations, requesting him to bring it to the attention of the Soviet government.[2]

As the Memorandum began to attract publicity in the West, the Soviet authorities reacted by trying to hunt down those responsible. They also exerted pressure in a different direction. On 11 April, the same Rugienis summoned the bishops and administrators of the Lithuanian Church to a meeting in the Kaunas Archdiocesan Curia. Here they were presented with a 'Pastoral Letter'[3] for signature. It was addressed to all Lithuanian Catholics and appealed for unity within the Church. In only slightly veiled terms it condemned the organized circulation of 'irresponsible documents'. This 'Pastoral Letter' was then circulated to all priests with instructions that it be read on 30 April, in place of the normal Sunday sermon. On that day, two state officials were present in each church to observe what happened.

Outraged at this manoeuvre, a number of priests combined to write a reply to this 'Pastoral Letter' dated May 1972.[4] They condemned the hierarchy for allowing this state of affairs to prevail. They refuted the accusations contained in the bishops' letter and declared: 'We have had enough of these Monsignori who spread the "truth" about the Lithuanian Catholic Church by means of the atheist radio and press. We have also had enough of the kind of bishops who publish such "pastoral" letters . . . Help us with your prayers and tell the world that we want at the present time only as much freedom of conscience as is permitted by the Constitution of the Soviet Union. We are full of determination, for God is with us.'

The situation of the Catholics in Lithuania is perhaps unique because of the broad base of support among both people and clergy for such bold declarations as that just quoted. This is certainly due in part to the strong national ties of this Church; more recent numbers of the *Chronicle* have given greater space to events of a more purely nationalist character, thus emphasizing this unique link. However, it appears that even the hierarchs, who came in for such strong criticism in 1972, have changed their attitude somewhat. *Chronicle* No. 6 relates that one priest wrote to Mgr Labukas and the other bishops to complain about current church–state relations. One of the bishops—the *Chronicle* does not name him—

[2] English in G. Simon, *Church, State and Opposition in the Soviet Union*, London 1974, pp. 234–7.
[3] English in *The Tablet*, London, 5 August, 1972, pp. 749–50.
[4] English in *The Tablet*, London, 6 January, 1973, pp. 21–2.

replied in sympathetic terms and expressed his hope that Lithuania might attain to that 'normalization' of relations such as prevailed in 'Poland, Hungary and other socialist countries'.[5]

Despite many attempts by the authorities to persuade the bishops to issue a statement denouncing the *Chronicle of the Lithuanian Catholic Church*, no such denunciation appeared. Instead, the bishops themselves issued a guarded criticism of the new Soviet Constitution for implied discrimination against religious believers, which was published in no. 33 of the *Chronicle*.

The state authorities at first tried to stamp out further petitions and 'unofficial' journals by force. At the beginning of 1973 it was demanded that samples of all typewriters be submitted to the authorities in an obvious attempt to stamp out further petitions. This action led to the arrest in 1973–4 of several persons, some for producing religious literature and others for circulating the *Chronicle*. Four men, P. Plumpa, V. Jaugelis, P. Petronis and J. Stasaitis, were tried in December 1974 and sentenced to terms of imprisonment ranging from one year to eight years (*Guardian*, 31 December 1974, based on an article in *Sovetskaya Litva* (Soviet Lithuania), 29 December 1974).

These trials were followed by others, although it became more and more clear that such repression would not close down the *Chronicle*—indeed it has given birth to seven or eight other 'unofficial' journals, mostly of a religious character. In 1975, Nijole Sadunaite and Juozas Gražys were tried for helping to produce the *Chronicle* and sentenced to three years imprisonment, followed by three years of exile in Siberia. More trials followed: those of Ona Pranskunaite (1977), Viktoras Petkus (1978) and Balys Gajauskas (1978). Petkus and Gajauskas received extremely severe sentences of fifteen years and exile. Their trials were reported in subsequent issues of the *Chronicle*.

Nevertheless, the writing of petitions continued unabated. *Chronicle* No. 6 includes the texts of an appeal to Mr Brezhnev signed by no less than 30,782 people. It was accompanied by two other petitions, one dealing with discrimination against believing children in the schools and the other with the lamentable state of religious literature in the Lithuanian Church. The latter was signed by 16,498 people and the former by 14,284 of whom about a quarter were young people. The *Chronicle* gives some graphic

[5] ELTA-Press, No. 9, 1973, p. 13.

details of how such multitudes of signatures are gathered despite police vigilance.[6]

A new petition calling for the return of the Catholic church built by believers in Kalipeda and confiscated by the authorities in 1960, is said to bear 148,000 signatures.[7]

The question of religious versus atheist education of children is indeed crucial for the Lithuanian believers. Their appeals tell of vulgar attacks on religion in the schools, but also of the spirited defence put up by parents and by the children themselves. One atheist teacher was told that since Lenin was her god, she should go and worship him in Moscow and leave the Lithuanian Catholics in peace.

This determined and uncompromising mood of the believers is also revealed in the continuing existence of the *Chronicle*, despite 'governmental repressions', and in the support shown by priests and laymen for the Catholic Committee for the Defence of Believers' Rights. This committee was founded in November 1978, on the lines of the earlier Russian Christian Committee, by five priests: Frs Zdebskis, Kauneckas, Tamkevičius, Svarinskas and Velavičius. It has now issued over twenty documents highlighting various aspects of believers' rights in the USSR, concentrating on Catholic believers but including some Pentecostals. During the International Year of the Child, the Catholic Committee sent a document to UNESCO protesting against the violation of children's religious rights in Lithuania. The extent of its support among the clergy is shown in collective letters written by 522 priests of all dioceses (a majority of the 711 in Lithuania) in the spring of 1979. These letters defended the point of view put forward in the Catholic Committee's Document No. 5, which denounced the Soviet Constitution and laws as discriminatory and biased, making it impossible for believers to observe them fully.

The reaction of the Soviet authorities to this large-scale involvement of the clergy in an open protest movement has been somewhat unsure. Since 1975, no priests have been sent to prison, though many have been fined or harassed. The Catholic Committee have been threatened with prosecution and may yet be arrested, but are so far continuing their activities and even openly celebrated Mass together at the shrine of Šiluva in 1979.

Lithuanian Catholics have been greatly encouraged by the elec-

[6] ELTA-Press, No. 9, 1973, p. 4–8.
[7] USSR News Brief, 2/1980.

tion of the Polish Pope, John Paul II, and his words of support to them. Although the border to Poland was more or less closed during the Pope's visit there, many Lithuanians close to the Polish border watched it on TV.

DOCUMENT 19:
THE CATHOLIC COMMITTEE FOR THE DEFENCE OF BELIEVERS'
RIGHTS DOCUMENT NO. 5
23 DECEMBER 1978

To: The USSR Presidium of the Supreme Soviet
The LSSR Presidium of the Supreme Soviet
Bishops of Diocesan Administrations of Lithuania
The Chairman of the Council for Religious Affairs (CRA),
P. Anilionis

Thirty years ago, on 10 December 1948, the UN General Assembly accepted the Universal Declaration of Human Rights, which the Soviet Union also undertook to implement faithfully by its signature. The Soviet press even asserts that the new USSR Constitution guarantees a great deal more rights and freedoms than those visualized in the Universal Declaration of Human Rights.

The Catholics of Lithuania, having experienced various forms of discrimination in the post-war years, hoped that on the occasion of the illustrious jubilee of the Universal Declaration of Human Rights the Soviet government would accord them at least a few more rights and freedoms, but the opposite happened instead. On 24 November 1978 the Chairman of the Council for Religious Affairs (CRA), P. Anilionis, summoned all of Lithuania's bishops and diocesan administrators to Vilnius and firmly emphasized that from now on it would be necessary to abide by the Regulations on Religious Associations confirmed by the Presidium of the LSSR Supreme Soviet on 28 July 1976, and that if this were not done severe penalties would ensue.

The Presidium of the LSSR Supreme Soviet in confirming the Regulations on Religious Associations should first have taken into account that the Catholic Church in Lithuania not only has 600 years of history and has incontrovertibly done much to benefit Lithuania (e.g. the foundation of Vilnius University by the Jesuits 400 years ago) but also the fact that even at the present time no less than seventy per cent of Lithuania's inhabitants belong to the

Catholic Church, and only an insignificant proportion regard themselves as atheists. The People's government, in confirming the Regulations, should have taken into account the convictions and will of the majority of citizens, but instead acted to the contrary; the interests of a handful of atheists decided the discriminatory nature of the Regulations on Religious Associations.

By means of this document we wish to turn the attention of the Soviet government to the way in which the priests and believers of Lithuania evaluate the Regulations thrust upon them. These Regulations contradict not only the Universal Declaration of Human Rights, but also the LSSR Constitution and aim to destroy the Catholic Church in Lithuania by administrative measures.

1.   The Regulations on Religious Associations require that a religious community [i.e. any group of believers—described as a 'religious association' in Soviet law] be registered (art. 2); without being registered it cannot embark on any activity (art. 4). In order to register a religious community a request has to be made to the executive committee of the district (or town) *soviet* of People's Deputies, which arrives at a decision and then sends the request, together with its conclusions, to the LSSR Council of Ministers (art. 5). The latter considers the material sent to it (art. 7) and sends it on to the CRA attached to the USSR Council of Ministers, which either registers the religious community or rejects its request (art. 4).

The Regulations which require a religious community to register do not guarantee that it will be registered. In fact the registration of a religious community can be prevented by the executive committee of a district *soviet*, a republic's Council of Ministers and the CRA. A religious community can be harassed for years on end as regards registration, and be left in the dark as to the person responsible. It does not even have the right to complain to a People's Court about the actions of local government officials. On 31 March 1978 the believers of Žalioji (Vilkaviškis district), having made numerous unsuccessful attempts to have their community registered, appealed to the CRA in Moscow to register their community. The Council sent the appeal of the Žalioji religious community to the Chairman of the CRA in Vilnius, and the latter turned the whole of the matter over to the executive committee of the Vilkaviškis district *soviet* whose representative, J. Urbonas, declared that the Žalioji religious community would never be registered. Similarly, in 1976–7 the Slabadai (Vilkaviškis district) religious community endeavoured in vain to obtain registration and to start its activities; it constantly found itself confronted with the arbitrariness of government officials.

If, in accordance with the LSSR Constitution, the 'Church in the Lithuanian SSR is separated from the state', the state has no right to demand the registration of religious communities and should be content to be informed that such-and-such a community exists. The requirement that a religious community must register means that it is forbidden, and only registration confers upon it the right to exist. This is in direct contradiction to the Universal Declaration of Human Rights which proclaims that 'Each person has the right freely to . . . belong to organizations' (art. 20).

The Regulations allow membership of religious communities to be open only to those above the age of 18 (art. 3).

The Catholic Church has never agreed with this, and will never agree, for it is a basic contradiction of its teaching and its laws (canons). The Church, basing itself upon the teaching of Christ that baptism, penance and other sacraments are necessary for salvation, requires that babies be christened within a month and that children from about the age of seven go to confession and Holy Communion. The Church thus regards people as its members not from the age of 18, but from the date of their baptism. The state, therefore, in guaranteeing its citizens the 'freedom to practise cults' without reservations in its Constitution cannot revoke these guarantees or qualify them by its laws.

Regulations which specify that only from the age of 18 can persons be members of religious communities open the door wide to discrimination against believers. There is no guarantee, on the basis of art. 3 of the Regulations, that government officials will not one day begin to forbid the baptizing of babies, the admission of children to the sacraments or into a church itself, etc. The example of the RSFSR and other republics shows that this fear of the Lithuanian people has some foundation. For example, the Regulations on Religious Associations of the Latvian SSR even impose a direct ban on participation in religious rites to those under 18.

2. 'A religious community has the right to acquire church fittings, religious cult objects and means of transport, to rent, to erect and to buy buildings . . .' (art. 3).

In another section the Regulations assert that 'property essential for cult practices, whether it is transferred by agreement for the use of believers when the religious community is created or ob-

tained as gifts for cult purposes, is the property of the state . . .'
(art. 22). If a religious community is disbanded the State even takes
its funds, incense, candles, wine, wax and fuel (art. 34 'e'). This
means that the basic idea behind art. 3 is the following: a religious
community has the right, on behalf not of itself but of the state(!),
to acquire various church fittings and cult objects, means of transport, buildings, etc. The state, by confiscating the articles donated
by believers, coarsely violates the will of believers who, in making
donations to the Church, have no desire whatsoever to enrich state
or museum stocks; it does not abide by the Universal Declaration
which proclaims that 'property cannot arbitrarily be confiscated by
anyone' (art. 17–2).

Art. 10 of the Regulations states that a religious community
'may', in accordance with an established procedure, obtain a
special, single house of prayer. In other words, the believers may
not get such a house if this is against the wishes of local atheists
or government officials. Many churches have been arbitrarily
closed in Lithuania: in Vilnius, Kaunas, Klaipeda, Ukmerge, Panevežys and other places. Religious communities should have an
unfettered right to acquire or erect churches if they do not already
possess them. Since churches in Lithuania are built not by atheists,
but by the believers, the state is doing the believers no favour by
allowing them to be used. Similarly, the state cannot stipulate how
many prayer houses a religious community can have. This would
be a clear interference in the internal affairs of a religious
community.

3.   According to the Regulations, various functions within a religious community can only be carried out by 'separate
individuals', i.e. a religious community is not acknowledged as
having the right of legal personality. Collective farms, co-opera-
tives, hospitals, even art, sport and other societies may be regarded
as having the right of legal personality and only religious associations cannot. This means that Lithuanian believers (all believers
in the Soviet Union are in a similar situation) are not equal with
atheists before the law, and that the state, in fact, regards them as
second-class citizens even though the LSSR Constitution states that
'citizens of the Lithuanian SSR are equal before the law . . .' (art.
32).

4.   'General meetings of religious associations and groups of believers (other than religious services) take place . . . with the permission of an executive committee' [of a local *soviet*] (art. 12).

This means that not even a group of three or four believers can meet together to discuss their religious affairs without the permission of the district authorities. This article is contrary to the Universal Declaration of Human Rights which proclaims that 'every person has the right . . . to take part in peaceful meetings' (art. 20–1), and creates the impression that the state views believers as criminals whose every step has to be kept under scrutiny. Such Regulations artificially create dissatisfaction, distrust and opposition to the state amongst believers and this greatly hinders normal social development.

5. A religious association 'chooses its executive officials from its members by means of open elections held at general meetings of believers' (art. 13).

If 'the Church in the Lithuanian SSR is separated from the state' (art. 50 of the LSSR Constitution), then has the state the right to concern itself with how voting in religious communities is conducted—whether it be by secret or open ballot? Believers interpret the requirement that voting within religious communities is to be open as an effort by the state to prevent the election of suitable representatives for a religious community. Since the Regulations do not prevent government officials from taking part in a general meeting of a religious association, such officials can morally coerce the members of a religious community to elect persons desirable to the executive committee of the district *soviet* and not to the community.

If 'open voting' has not brought results and believers have chosen conscientious and active representatives for the religious community, the executive committee of the district *soviet* has the right arbitrarily to remove any person from the community's executive organs (art. 14). The atheist government thus desires to administer the Church and subordinate it to its requirements through the executive committees.

6. 'Religious associations do not have the right to organize meetings especially for children or young people . . .' (art. 17). 'The teaching of religion may only be permitted in theological schools . . .' (art. 18).

In schools believing pupils are forced to enrol in various atheist organizations, contrary to the Universal Declaration of Human Rights which declares that 'no one may be compelled to join any organization' (art. 20). Religious pupils have to take part in 'special' atheist, pioneer and Komsomol meetings, but they are forbidden to deepen their knowledge of religion by gathering together or even to learn to sing religious hymns—because all this is regarded

as 'special meetings'. Art. 17 of the Regulations is in direct contradiction to art. 20 of the Universal Declaration which guarantees
to every individual (be they children, school pupils or young persons) the right freely to participate in peaceful gatherings.

7.   Art. 18 of the Regulations speaks of 'religious schools' which,
in Lithuania, are forbidden, whilst the only seminary for priests
(Kaunas) is subject to strict limitations and is kept under the dili-
gent control of government officials. The Presidium of the LSSR
Supreme Soviet, by a decree of 12 May 1966, has forbidden the
religious instruction of schoolchildren. In reality this decree of the
Presidium of the Supreme Soviet is invalid, for it directly contradicts the international convention 'on the fight against discrimination in the sphere of education', which took effect in the Soviet
Union on 1 November 1962. Art. 6 of this convention stipulates
that parents must have the possibility of 'ensuring the religious or
moral education of children in accordance with the parents' own
convictions'. Arts. 17 and 18 of the Regulations deprive parents of
the possibility of ensuring such education. On the basis of the
decree of 12 May 1966 a number of priests in Lithuania—Juozas
Zdebskis, Prosperas Bubnys, Antanas Šeškevičius—were sentenced to imprisonment merely because, at the request of parents,
they had taught religious truths to children.

   According to art. 18, even a grandfather who talks about God
to his grandchildren can be prosecuted. Permission to teach religion
only in religious schools, which are themselves forbidden, is in
essence deceitful and conceals within itself the undertaking to root
out religion as quickly as possible. Art. 18 leaves open the future
possibility of banning the preaching of sermons by priests, as
preaching in churches is lecturing on religion outside a religious
school. Finally, art. 18 also contradicts the Universal Declaration
which gives every person 'the freedom to search for, obtain and
disseminate information and ideas by any means and irrespective
of state boundaries' (art. 19). Why then do the Regulations confine
religious teaching within any boundaries?

8.   Priests are only allowed to carry out religious rites within the
territory and church of the religious community which they serve
(art. 19).

   Christ ordered his disciples to go out, not to a religious community permitted by a state, but 'to the whole world' (Matt. 28:19)
and spread the Gospel to all—pagans, believers and atheists. Art.
19 forces priests to sin against their conscience, and it hinders
believers from fulfilling the obligations laid upon them by their

faith. For example, government officials, in preventing priests from helping one another during local church festivals, at the same time prevent believers from going to Easter confession and obtaining remission of their sins, and thus make a mockery of the 'freedom of cults' guaranteed by the LSSR Constitution. Art. 19 also contradicts the Universal Declaration which gives every person the right freely to disseminate his ideas 'irrespective of state boundaries' (art. 19), let alone of the boundaries of a religious community.

9. 'Religious centres and diocesan administrations are given the right to produce church fittings and necessities for a religious cult' (art. 20).

The right is given but the means are taken away and, therefore, throughout the whole of the post-war period not a single rosary has officially been made and not a single catechism issued. With the permission of the Soviet government, only a very limited number of prayer books has appeared, and this has been insufficient to satisfy the requirements of even one in a hundred believers.

10. Arts. 22 and 34 of the Regulations, by treating articles necessary for the performance of religious services as state property, allow government offices even to appropriate vessels used in the Holy Mass—chalices, monstrances, etc. Believers are made to fear that the state, by its laws, is legalizing such sacrilege. Believers are obliged by their consciences to protect holy vessels by all possible means from thieves; and the publishers of these Regulations are therefore responsible for provoking conflict and for causing millions of believers to take up anti-state positions. The paragraphs in question injure a believer's deepest feelings. Where then is this 'separation of the Church from the state' if the fingers of government officials even reach the holiest of holy places—the tabernacle of the altar?!

When a religious community is deprived of its property, then the Universal Declaration is infringed, which proclaims that 'every person has the right, alone or together with others, to own property' (art. 17). Believers will only become convinced that the state is not discriminating against the Church when religious communities are allowed to own property and to have the right of legal personality.

11. The Regulations permit a religious community to make use of a house of prayer and other cult property only if an agreement is made with the executive committee of the district *soviet* and only

if the religious community accepts the one-sided conditions thrust upon it (arts. 23, 24 and 25).

In 1948, during the Stalinist period, so-called 'agreements' were forced upon the Catholic Church in Lithuania. Believers were threatened with the closure of churches, while priests were persecuted. It is strange that in 1975 the Soviet government should repeat the injuries done to the Church during the Stalinist period and once more force 'agreements' on it. In fact, believers cannot freely accept 'agreements' which are one-sided and discriminate against believers, for they involve administrative interference by government officials in the internal life of the Church.

The Regulations even allow executive committee members of local *soviets* to check the Church and its property at any time (art. 24 'f'). This makes one think that under this cover government officials can, without any legal permit and at any time of the day or night (even midnight), conduct a search of a church—to 'check upon and inspect property', including the altar tabernacle where the Holy Sacrament is kept.

12. The Regulations allow for the eventual inclusion among a religious community's representatives (council of twenty) of people with appropriate beliefs and views (art. 27).

The Regulations thereby leave open the way for people with unclear motives to enter a religious community. The government may regard someone who was once baptized but is now an atheist and concerned only with defending the interests of the state, as being a person with 'appropriate views'. People of this kind, should they become a majority within a particular religious community, might even disrupt the community in question. In fact, only true believers, known to all, can create a religious community.

13. Insurance compensation for a house of prayer which has been burned down is given to the executive committee of the local *soviet*, which has the right to allocate money received for any purpose, even for atheist activity (art. 29). What discrimination against believers! They build churches, pay rents to the government for them, and do not receive the insurance payments in the event of an accident. Most often the religious community does not even get permission to build a new house of prayer. For example, in Sangruda (Kapsukas district), when the church was burned down the executive committee of the Kapsukas district *soviet* took the money and would not allow the religious community to build a new church. The believers had to make do with a residential building in which a wretched little house of prayer was installed.

There were similar occurrences in Batakiai, Gaure and other places. Art. 29 greatly encourages militant atheists to destroy churches deliberately, and believers in Lithuania suspect that the majority of the churches burned down in post-war years were subject to arson perpetrated by evil-doers.

14. The LSSR Council of Ministers has the unlimited right, irrespective of believers' wishes, to close a church at any time and to use it for secular purposes or even to demolish it and confiscate all its property and wealth (arts. 30, 31, 32, 33 and 34). A great wrong was done to believers in Lithuania in the post-war years when many churches were closed against the wishes of believers. These churches were then turned into store houses, workshops and even, in the case of the Church of St Casimir in Vilnius, into an atheist museum! Since a religious community does not have the right of legal personality, it is unable to use the processes of law to defend its rights. Believers therefore constantly live under the shadow of fear and have to submit to the arbitrary acts of local officials because their house of prayer is threatened with closure should they disobey.

It is sufficient for a local atheist council merely to complain that a religious community has infringed the law on cults (arts. 35 and 36) for the LSSR Council of Ministers to decide to close a church or abolish a religious community. A religious community therefore has not only to tremble before officials but also before the local atheists. Art. 35 of the Regulations is a sword of Damocles held constantly over the heads of believers.

The situation would be normal only if the activity of a religious community could be ended solely through a court of law, and only for a serious offence, and not for non-implementation of anti-constitutional Regulations.

15. Arts. 37–44 affirm that, even for the smallest of repairs to a church, a permit from the executive committee of the district *soviet* is required; that when any repairs are under way, which may sometimes last a year, services are not allowed to be held and that executive committees [of local *soviets*] can, on the basis of reports from commissions sent by them, decide to demolish a church. All this gives the atheist government wide scope for depriving believers of their churches under the pretext of repairs or the age of a building. Thus they use administrative methods in fighting against religion. But the Regulations do not mention any requirement on the part of the executive committee of district *soviets* to assist believers by at least giving them the necessary allocation of material

for church repairs. At the present time both organizations and individuals are afraid to help repair churches because this is regarded unofficially as being almost equivalent to anti-Soviet activity.

16. A religious community is allowed to collect donations only in a house of prayer (art. 45). This article is directly aimed at small religious communities. Since collective farm workers are often forced to work on Sundays and other believers are unable to go to church because of old age, or because of the long distances involved, or for other reasons, they are unable to contribute to the collections made for the maintenance of their church. The religious communities are thus hindered from obtaining sufficient funds for repairs, wages and, most important, the payment of the large rents imposed upon them (for taxes, insurance, etc.).

17. Religious communities do not have the right to establish mutual aid funds (art. 45 'd').

This ban is contrary to the commandment of Christ to do good to people, and thus forbids believers to live in accordance with the requirements of Christian love. Religious communities are not even allowed to give material aid to their members (art. 45). The state does not accept into trade unions those directly employed in church work (priests, organists, sacristans) and does not give them pensions in their old age. Arts. 32 and 41 of the Constitution are not valid for them. For example, priests in Lithuania pay large sums in taxes each year but have no right to material aid in their old age. That religious communities are forbidden to give material aid to their members is inhuman, and amounts to an order that servants of the Church have the right only to deprivation and hunger in their old age. Believers see this article as an attempt by the atheist government to frighten believers away from serving the Church.

18. Priests are forbidden to visit parishioners for the collection of alms (art. 45).

Church law requires priests to visit all of their parishioners each year. Regulations forbidding a priest to visit his parishioners aim at isolating him from the community. A priest is thus forbidden not only to work in other parishes but even to carry out his essential duties in his own parish.

19. Every article donated to a church, e.g. a carpet, chalice, etc., must be entered in the inventory (art. 46) and becomes state property. In donating something to a church, believers have not the

slightest intention of giving the article to the state. This article is clearly discriminatory and serves to dissuade believers from supporting and beautifying the church with their donations.

20. A priest is allowed to visit a person gravely ill in hospital (art. 49), but this concession is constantly being restricted because, on the orders of the executive committee of district *soviets*, doctors very often forbid priests to visit patients, ostensibly because the patient is not yet dying or because there is no separate accommodation where the priest might perform his religious ministrations. Art 49 impermissibly restricts the right to 'freedom of cults' guaranteed by the LSSR Constitution.

21. Special permission from the executive committee of a district *soviet* is required for religious processions and rites in the open air (art. 50).

If atheists have the right to organize processions, festivals and various civil celebrations in public places, then believers should have equivalent rights. Throughout the post-war period, however, not a single religious community of Lithuania has been given permission for a religious procession beyond church grounds (an exception is made only for the funeral of a priest).

22. Art. 50 forbids priests to hold religious services in the apartments of believers, e.g. the baptism of a sick child, the blessing of a house, etc. Believers regard this ban as anti-constitutional interference in the privacy of a citizen's home and the affairs of his conscience. This article even forbids three or four believers to pray together in a field, a forest, even in the privacy of believers' homes without permission from the executive committee of the local *soviet*. Religious rites can only be performed at the request of a person gravely ill or dying. The executive committee is thus given the right to decide when a person is truly gravely ill or dying. In the territory of the Moldavian SSR, for example, it is demanded that a doctor supply written evidence to the effect that a patient is truly gravely ill, and only then can the priest hope to get the executive committee's permission to visit the patient.

If the Soviet government compels priests and believers to abide by these anti-human, anti-constitutional Regulations, which contradict the Universal Declaration of Human Rights and other international agreements made by the USSR, dissension will be created within the nation and millions of believers will feel themselves to be wronged and denigrated. We therefore ask the Presidium of the Supreme Soviet of the USSR and the LSSR, for the reasons outlined above, to repeal these Regulations as quickly as possible.

Members of the Catholic Committee for
the Defence of Believers' Rights (CCDBR)
Fr Jonas Kauneckas
Fr Alfonsas Svarinskas
Fr Sigitas Tamkevičius
Fr Vincas Velavičius
Fr Juozas Zdebskis

(b) EASTERN-RITE CATHOLICS

Eastern-rite Catholics, also known as Greek Catholics and Uniates, are found in many parts of Eastern Europe where Orthodox Christians came under Catholic rule and agreed to accept the primacy of Rome while retaining many features of Orthodox ritual and practice, such as a Slavonic liturgy and married parish clergy. They remain a point of contention between Orthodox and Catholics. After the Second World War most Eastern-rite Catholics were forced to accept amalgamation with national Orthodox churches. This was the case in the Soviet Union where the Church is mostly represented in Western Ukraine, annexed in 1939. Unrepresentative church councils in Lvov in 1946 and Uzhgorod in 1949 resolved under state pressure to 'return' to the Russian Orthodox Church. Most of the clergy who rejected this move (such as then Archbishop, now Cardinal Josif Slypij) were arrested at this time. Others agreed to continue parish work as Orthodox priests at the same time remaining secretly loyal to their Church and maintaining contacts. The faithful were similarly divided between those who took part in Orthodox parish life and remained Catholic at heart and those who began to organize clandestine worship. At the present time several bishops and several hundred clergy are believed to be working secretly in Western Ukraine. Many of the three million or so believers living in the area in the period before the Church was dissolved are thought to be still loyal to their Catholic traditions, both as secret Catholics in Orthodox parishes and in the clandestine congregations.

Very little news of this Church leaks out of the Soviet Union. Documents by the believers describing their own situation are not available. Occasionally reports emerge of arrests or other prisoners write of fellow inmates from the Eastern-rite Church. A number of priests are in this way known to be serving sentences for performing their duties; nuns are in prison for organizing secret convents; lay-people have been arrested for clandestine production of liturgical books and other literature.

The Ukrainian Eastern-rite Catholic Church therefore lives under the greatest possible degree of restriction: a total ban on its activities. Although some Protestant and Orthodox minorities also share this fate, the Eastern-rite Catholics are the largest denomination in the Soviet Union that is completely outlawed.

V.

Other Faiths

(a) JEWS

In scarcely any case is the religious problem so closely bound up with the national one as with the Jewish minority in the USSR.

During the last twenty years the situation for religious Jews has progressively deteriorated, though less rapidly since 1966. Had the rate of decline remained constant, then, as the synagogue statistics set out below illustrate, there would have long since been no synagogues whatsoever in the Soviet Union. These figures are based on a table quoted in the periodical *Russia Cristiana* (Milan, January 1970, pp. 53–4). They would seem to be a reasonably accurate estimate of the number of open synagogues, except possibly for the discrepancy between the 1956 and 1960 totals. The latter comes from a Moscow Radio broadcast of 22 July 1960, which, if accurate, may mean that the former is too high. It seems more likely that Moscow Radio's figure was too low, so there would have been more closures in the early 1960s.

1917	3,000 (approximately)
1941	1,011
July 1956	450
July 1960	150
February 1964	97
July 1964	92
1966	62
1969	40–50

A Soviet source in 1976 put the total number of registered synagogues at 92, a figure which he said had remained constant for twelve years. There are also believed to be about 300 groups meeting for prayer in private houses.

Eighteen of the synagogues are in Georgia alone, although only 2·5 per cent of the Jewish population lives there. Seventeen more are in the Asiatic part of the USSR and in parts of the Caucasus outside Georgia. This means that almost half of all the synagogues are in the non-Russian parts of the Soviet Union, in areas containing less than 10 per cent of the Soviet Jewish population. The region of Birobidjan, designated by Stalin as an area to which Jews would be moved, is almost completely secularized and has no synagogues at all, as far as is known.

Even if these statistics should prove to be not entirely accurate, we have documented information from Soviet sources about this progressive decline, as well as certain events which were reported by eye-witnesses. It was reported, for example, that when the campaign against Jews was intensifying, the synagogues of Malakhovka (near Moscow) and Tskhakaya (Georgia) were burned down in 1959 and 1962 respectively. Money collected by Soviet Jews to build new synagogues was confiscated by the authorities. Extreme pressure was exerted against those who attempted to exploit their legal right of forming councils of twenty (*dvadtsatki*) and petitioning for the opening of synagogues, which meant that Jewish congregations were deprived of the one freedom which Lenin had unambiguously bequeathed to religious people.

Leningradskaya Pravda (Leningrad Truth) on 11 November 1961 reported the sentencing of three members of the Leningrad synagogue to four, seven and twelve years' imprisonment. They were accused of having contacts with Westerners and of having furnished the latter with 'anti-Soviet' material. In 1962 the Lvov synagogue was closed after a series of attacks in the Soviet press. The press campaign against religious Jews went so far as to assert that some had been guilty of ritual murder.

Since the Six-Day War in 1967 there has been a general hardening of domestic policy as an inevitable corollary of the extreme anti-Israeli position of the Soviet government. Reports reached the West in 1976 of harassment of Jews attending Passover synagogue services in Moscow. In one town in Moldavia, Jews had been meeting for worship in a private house since their synagogue was closed in 1961; but in 1976 they were told that these services would no longer be permitted. In 1979 a Jew was arrested in Tashkent for engaging in an illegal trade: the baking and selling of matzos. Any sectors of the population with anti-semitic instincts believe that they can give vent to them with impunity under such circumstances. Anti-semitism is frequently condoned by Soviet officials and even promoted in official publications under the cloak of anti-Zionism.

In 1964, T. K. Kichko's book *Judaism without Embellishment*

(Kiev) was published. Its anti-semitic tone aroused protest from some Western Communist Parties and it was eventually officially condemned in the USSR also. Yet a brochure by Y. Ivanov, *Beware! Zionism* (Moscow, 1968, second edition 1970) has, not unjustly, been compared by Russian and foreign Jews to the notorious *Protocols of the Elders of Zion*. More recent anti-Zionist works with a markedly anti-semitic flavour are *Creeping Counter-Revolution* (Minsk, 1974) and *Invasion Without Arms* (Moscow, 1977), both by Vladimir Begun.

Today religious Judaism has been reduced to its lowest point in Soviet history. There are probably no more than 35–40 active rabbis. Soviet sources claim that there are some 50,000 religious Jews in the USSR; but others believe that there are as many as 250,000. Moscow has a quarter to half a million Jewish inhabitants—the largest number in any city of the world after New York—yet it has only one of its former eleven synagogues and two small prayer houses remaining open. The only *yeshiva* (theological school) in existence in the USSR is attached to the Moscow synagogue, but doubts have frequently been expressed as to the reality of its functioning. However, early in 1974 western sources learned of the expulsion of one of the few pupils, Ilya Essas, following his application to emigrate to Israel (*Jews in the USSR*, London, 15 March 1974, p.2); and in 1976 a western visitor reported that the *yeshiva* was operating, albeit with only half a dozen students and to a low academic standard. Some Soviet Jews are able to go abroad for training as rabbis. In 1974, it was announced that ten young men would receive rabbinical training at the Budapest Jewish Theological Seminary (see *Religion in Communist Lands*, vol. ii, nos. 4–5, pp. 56–7).

Soviet Judaism found its voice in the early 1970s. A large number of petitions began reaching the West, mostly addressed to the U.N. and the Israeli government. In these, Soviet citizens asked for active support for their attempts to emigrate to Israel. In many of these letters there is direct reference to religious discrimination: almost all the documents describe the struggle of the Soviet authorities against Jewish traditions that are thousands of years old. A number of these appeals were published in the journal *Iskhod* ('Exodus')—modelled on the clandestine organ, *Chronicle of Current Events*—the first number of which began to circulate in April 1970. This journal did not last long, but was replaced by others. In October 1972 the journal *Evrei v SSSR* ('Jews in the USSR') began to appear, with the names and addresses of its editors openly displayed on the title page. It includes articles on Jewish religion, history and culture. From 1975 it included a supplement called *Tarbut* ('Culture'), which since 1976 has been flourishing as a separate journal, with an increasingly religious content.

When the greetings of seven Moscow Jews for Rosh Hashanah reached the American Jewish Congress in September 1970, this was probably the first letter from Soviet citizens to an American Jewish organization. They wrote:

> We are approaching the New Year with the confidence that in spite of the attempt to deprive us of our Jewishness and forcing us to live in, for us, an alien country, we will attain our rights to live in what is to us the holy land, the Land of Israel. And we repeat our centuries-old words with a renewed feeling of reality: 'Next year in Jerusalem' (*Jewish Chronicle*, 9 October 1970).

Recently there has been a lessening in the volume of Jewish *Samizdat*, since nearly all information is now communicated to the West by telephone.

Large-scale Jewish emigration began in 1971; and by the end of 1979 about 200,000 Jews had left the USSR. A certain proportion of those who apply for visas have their applications turned down. They are known as *refuseniks*.

Refuseniks, whether religious or non-religious, tend to gather outside the Moscow synagogue on Saturday afternoons, after the weekly service, to discuss their latest news. They have been criticized and even called 'hooligans' by worshippers in the synagogue. There is evidence of a revival of interest in religion amongst young Jews, particularly *refuseniks*. They do not attend the synagogue, but hold Jewish seminars and classes to learn Hebrew (which is not officially taught in the USSR) and to study religious texts. There are reports of two unofficial Jewish religious schools; and in 1979 came a report that Ilya Essas (see above) was now a member of an unofficial 'underground' *yeshiva*.

Of all religious (and of course ethnic) minorities in the Soviet Union, the Jews are those whose destiny is worst affected by their government's external policies. These, in their turn, may be partly affected by the worst side of Russian and Ukrainian nationalism. It is hard to foresee any substantial improvement while the Soviet 'anti-Zionist' campaign continues. It should be noted, however, that an increasing number of intellectuals dissociate themselves from anti-semitism in any form.

DOCUMENT 20:
LETTER TO RABBI LEVIN

This letter was written by forty-two Moscow Jews to the—now deceased—
Rabbi Levin, after he had made a statement condemning the Soviet Jewish
movement for emigration.

To the Rabbi of the Moscow Choral Synagogue
Rabbi Yehuda Levin[1]
You surely realize the main purpose of the Moscow authorities
who forcibly disperse from the gates of the Moscow synagogue
Jews struggling to emigrate to Israel.

We don't think you are convinced that everything which officials
have written, and read to us in your name last Sabbath near the
synagogue, is true. This piece of paper is similar in character to all
other statements published in your name in the Soviet press. It
seems to us that there is an obvious contradiction between the
Torah and your participation in such actions.

In our sacred books it is said that to live in the land of Israel is
equal to all the other commandments of the Torah.

You have also frequently preached that in every Jew there is a
divine spark. Rabbi, if someone in your situation is, with great
heartache, losing the love of so many Jews, it is obvious that he
is behaving this way because he, an old man, has not enough
strength to act otherwise.

But the greatest sin is to be dishonest with yourself. Rabbi Hillel
said: 'Don't separate yourself from the community, do not judge
your neighbour until you have been in his situation, and don't say
anything that should not be heard, because one day it will be
heard.' Rabbi, think of yourself, of your life, and for what purpose
you are wasting the spiritual strength given you by God.

On the eve of Rosh Hashanah, we want to remind you of the
words of a prayer which for a long time has not been uttered
within the Moscow synagogue: 'O God and God of our Fathers,
sound the great Shofar of our freedom, lift up the banner to gather
in our exiles, and bring together those who are dispersed among
the peoples, gather together our scattered ones from the far corners
of the earth, and bring them to Your city.'

Signed by 42 Jews
Moscow, 19 September, 1971

[1] This translation published in *Religion in Communist–Dominated Areas*, vol. x. nos.
15–18, pp. 145–6.

DOCUMENT 21:
JEWISH 'PRESS CONFERENCE'

In February 1972, a group of ninety-two Latvian Jews requested official permission to hold a press conference to present the views of many Soviet Jews on a range of critical questions. This appeal was made as a result of the numerous officially-sponsored 'press conferences' at which Soviet Jewish figures condemned Zionism and the emigration movement. Permission was refused, but the group were invited to submit their statements in writing, which they did in the following month. The following are two statements on the subject: 'Difficulties faced by Jews in the USSR in the observance of their religion'.[2]

1. *Answer by G. Branover, Professor, Doctor of Physics and Mathematics, Riga, Gorkogo 145, Apt. 34*
I wish to explain the problem I encounter as a religious Jew, to examine briefly what difficulties generally obstruct the observance of Jewish religious precepts in the Soviet Union, and to explain why my religious beliefs are the main motive for the fact that I am petitioning to emigrate.[3]

As is known, constant study of Torah and the teaching of the Torah to one's children is one of the main Jewish commandments, often equalled in importance to all the other commandments combined. But what possibilities do I have to give my child a religious education and upbringing? Apart from the fact that there are no proper educational institutions, any sort of tutoring in this sphere has long been forbidden. If I should wish to withdraw my child from school and teach him myself, the law providing for the obligatory attendance of schools by children exludes this, too.

At present in the USSR there is no possibility to obtain various essential articles necessary to believers . . . The receipt of such articles from other countries is forbidden by Soviet customs regulations. The observance of the laws concerning kosher food is made extremely difficult. Sick and elderly people often do not have sufficient physical strength to make long trips to obtain fowl and are forced to limit themselves to vegetarian food. Even so, in cases where they observe strict *kashrut*, they have to bake their own

---

[2] This translation was published in *Jews in Eastern Europe*, April 1972, pp. 52–4.
[3] Dr Branover is now in Israel. For extracts from his book *Iz Glubin* ('De Profundis') published in New York, see *Religion in Communist Lands*, vol. ii, no. 3, 1974. 21–3.

bread and the like. Religious people who are patients in hospitals are in an especially difficult position with regard to food. An insoluble problem faces those who find it necessary to end their marriage in accordance with religious laws. This can only be done by a rabbi, and to register the documents it is also necessary to have a 'shoifer'. But there is neither a rabbi nor shoifer in all the Baltic Republics, Belorussia and even at present in Moscow.[4]

These examples show that, despite the proclaimed freedom of religion, the strict observance of Jewish religious precepts is practically impossible in the Soviet Union. I have no desire to renounce my faith. On the contrary, I consider it my duty to explain to people in general, and to Jews in particular, that the widespread view of this so-called scientific age that religion is an anachronism, is a catastrophic mistake.

It is absurd, therefore, for the press to ascribe political, mercantile and various other motives to the longing of Jews to go to Israel.

2. *Answer by Grivsky, 60, Clerk, Riga, Runnietsibas 7, Apt. 9.*
Religious rites accompany a believer from the first day of his life to the last. A boy is born and on the eighth day afterwards the rite of circumcision is supposed to take place. Here begin the trials and tribulations of the infant and his parents. In the entire territory of the Baltic Republics and Belorussia, there remains only one seventy-year old man able to carry out religious circumcision. To take another example, the moment the kosher butcher leaves the boundaries of Riga, hundreds of religious people remain without meat. Within a few years this man, the only surviving master of his trade, will be unable to work because of old age, and then the believers will be totally deprived of any possibility of observing rites guaranteed by the Soviet Constitution. Jewish religious functionaries are not trained anywhere in the USSR,[5] so the Jewish religion is doomed to die out because of circumstances that have arisen and contrary to the desire of thousands of believers.

For all nationalities, even the smallest, there exist schools, textbooks are published, teachers are trained. I want to ask this question: In what school, according to what textbooks, can I teach my grandson to read and write in Hebrew, so that he should know the culture of his people, its history and the laws of its religion?

---

[4] In June 1972, Rabbi Yaakov Fishmann was appointed Rabbi of the Moscow synagogue.
[5] Cf. information cited in this section

Why do all other peoples have this possibility, whereas it is denied to me? Why am I degraded and discriminated against?

In the numerous Jewish communities of the large city of Riga, there is only one place of religion. On premises comprising about 200 square metres there have been squeezed a synagogue, the pool for ritual baths, and the slaughter house for fowls. There are many such examples. They show clearly that, in spite of the freedom of religion proclaimed in words, everything is done so that believers should not be able satisfactorily to carry out these rites and prayers according to the dictates of their hearts, their conscience and their reasons.

(b) MUSLIMS

The Muslim population of the Soviet Union is largely concentrated in the Central Asian republics, with other groups in the Caucasus, Bashkiria and the Kazan area.

The official Muslim administration consists of four *muftiats* in Ufa, Tashkent, Baku and Makhach-Kala. They administer some 300–500 registered mosques, about 1,000 registered clerics and two medressehs (in Bukhara and Tashkent) with perhaps 60–80 students. Official Islam adopts an extremely loyal attitude to the regime: recently, for example, a preacher in a Moscow mosque redefined the 'jihad' or Holy War as a war to construct a life based on socialist principles. Nevertheless, since the 1920s the authorities have been waging a ceaseless violent campaign against Islam.

A traveller in the USSR in 1976 reported that according to a representative of the Tashkent *muftiat* there were 146 working mosques in Central Asia and Kazakhstan (compared with more than 12,000 before 1914). In Daghestan-Chechnia, there were 27 mosques in 1967 (compared with 2,060 in Daghestan alone before 1914). In the Tatar country, there are now some 20 mosques (compared with 2,200 in 1927).

Science and Religion, in September 1963 (p. 75) stated that there were eighteen mosques and 69 imams (registered) for the whole of the Tadzhik republic (population 1½ million in 1959); in January the following year it said that there were no more than 39 imams working there officially (p. 22). In other words, nearly half of the imams had been barred from religious activity within a four-month period. It is well known, however, that such direct action merely drives religious activity underground. Anti-religious literature reveals the existence of a 'non-official' popular Islam, based on Sufi brotherhoods, with clandestine mosques, holy places of pilgrimage and secret Koranic schools run by 'unaccredited' clerics. For instance in Azerbaijan in 1969 there were said to be only 16 registered mosques but about 1,000 clandestine mosques. There

were also 300 places of pilgrimage. According to a Soviet estimate
in 1975, '. . . more than half the total number of believers and
almost all clerics in the North Caucasus today belong to a Sufi
brotherhood'. It is said that this 'non-official' Islam has in some
ways lost a great deal of its purity, containing much that has
survived in popular forms from pre-Islamic cults and beliefs; but
at the same time it imposes an iron discipline and interprets strictly
all the traditional Islamic duties. It wages a 'jihad' against the
Russian authorities—not in the name of 'human rights', but because the Russians are 'foreign infidels'.[1]

Press treatment of the Muslims is chiefly directed to accusations
about harmful traditions that have survived amongst Muslim
groups. There is, for example, the Muslim attitude to women:
frequent attacks are made on the practice of *kalym* (enforced payment for dowry). In 1975 the Supreme Court of Turkmenistan
reintroduced into its penal code an article making the practice of
kaitarma (keeping a bride in her parents' home until the dowry is
paid) punishable by up to two years in prison.

Another recurrent theme is the blood-feuds allegedly demanded
by Islam—the shedding of blood to wipe out a first offence, and
so on through generations. This custom is apparently still strong,
according to the Soviet press, among the Checheno-Ingush people.
It is often said in the press that Muslim rituals do not favour
hygiene and health. One significant article in *Science and Religion*
(March 1970, pp. 62–6) lists various diseases that may be contracted
through the observance of different rituals, including syphilis, ma-
laria, arteriosclerosis and cancer. This is even worse than the accusations that have been made against Baptists that multiple
baptisms are unhygienic!

Another fact that must be mentioned in this context, is the cruel
treatment of the Crimean Tatars. This ancient people's home, the
Crimea, belongs to the traditionally Muslim lands of the USSR.
In 1944 they were deported *en masse* by Stalin, who accused them
of having collaborated with the Nazis. Many of them died on the
way to Central Asia under the appalling conditions of the journey.
Since then, the survivors—numbering now over 300,000—have
been consistently denied the right to return to their old homeland.
Their traditional religious practices have been curtailed and they

---

[1]   See 'Muslim Religious Conservatism and Dissent in the USSR', by Alexandre
Bennigsen and Chantal Lemercier-Quelquejay, *Religion in Communist Lands*, vol.
vi, no. 3, pp. 153–61; 'Unofficial Islam: a Muslim Minority in the USSR', by
John Soper, *RCL*, vol. vii, no. 4, pp. 226–31.

have protested about this—but this, as with the Jews, is a case of discrimination being practised against a whole ethnic group. In 1978 Mussa Mamut, a Crimean Tatar, immolated himself in front of policemen in protest against the treatment of his people; and Mustafa Dzhemilev, one of the Crimean Tatars' leaders, who had already served several terms in prison, was sentenced in 1979 to four years' exile. A second group of Muslims, the Meskhetian Turks, were also deported in 1944 from their home in Georgia. They too have had their requests to return constantly turned down.

All this raises the important question of where religion ends and national entity begins. An article in *Science and Religion* of April 1967 has expressed this difficulty well: 'A word (Muslim) which indicates religious adherence is being used to define a group of nationalities, among whom this religion was once widely spread' (p. 50); and again: 'An incorrect idea of the word Muslim not only complicates the process of the withering away of religious rituals and customs, but also opens up loopholes for ideas of nationalism and panislamism' (p. 51). This is an unusually frank treatment of a crucial point. The dilemma of the Soviet authorities with regard to Islam has been well defined by Janis Sapiets 'Soviet policy towards Muslims is determined by two basic considerations: on the one hand, to convince foreign Muslims of Soviet friendship for Islam, and, on the other, to bring the day nearer when there will be no more Muslims left in the Soviet Union, because they will all have been "liberated from their religion", as the communists say. To reconcile these two aims requires a certain amount of ideological acrobatics. . .' This is apparent in the Soviet article mentioned above, and indeed the author seems to be aware of it towards the end, when he remarks: 'In recent years our links with Arab countries have become significantly stronger. I have heard from those who have been there that they easily found a common language with the population of these countries: "As soon as they discovered that we were Muslims, our relations became most warm". Without wanting to say anything bad about our Arab friends, I would, nevertheless, like to point out that it did not become representatives of a socialist country to look to religious adherence as a basis for friendship between nations' (p. 52).

To appear as champions of religious liberty in the Middle East and in Orthodox communities, while sounding the death-knell for religion at home, will continue to involve the Soviet authorities in the most complicated ideological manoeuvres.

DOCUMENT 22:
OPEN LETTER TO MUHAMMED ALI, THREE TIMES WORLD
CHAMPION

Reshat Dzhemilev is a Crimean Tatar active in the campaign to return to their homeland in the Crimea. He has already served one period of imprisonment for his activities and is at present again under arrest. The Crimean Tatars, a Muslim people, are primarily concerned to win the right to live in the Crimea, but they are also concerned about the preservation of their culture, which is moulded by Islam. In respect of their religion, they face the same problems and restrictions as all other Muslim peoples of the Soviet Union, as the following document illustrates.

Dear Mr Ali,
I have before me a copy of the journal *Za rubezhom* published weekly in the USSR, no. 45 for 1978, where there is an article by Marilyn Bichtell a correspondent of *New World Review*. Ms Bichtell goes into some detail about your impressions of a ten-day trip to the Soviet Union which you made at the invitation of the Committee on physical culture and sport. . . .

In your impressions you touched upon many problems and apparently are trying not only to convince the public of your country and of the West of the correctness of your conclusions, but also to assure of their correctness us, Soviet citizens who learnt to appreciate with our mothers' milk 'freedom of speech and of the press', 'respect for small nations', 'anti-racism', 'absence of envy and of suspicion', etc. I agree with you that 'it is a country with a great history'. But to know its history you must study it; and not in the way that Angela Davis did in 1972—from the windows of a car racing through the streets of towns and villages at a terrific speed, accompanied by militia and KGB agents—but in such a way that you could freely approach any citizen, as Soviet journalists and correspondents do in the West, and ask for answers to all your questions without anyone being afraid or looking over his shoulder to see if anybody is eavesdropping so that he will not be sent to prison for 'divulging state secrets' or for 'slandering the Soviet state and social system'. . .

Yes, you are right, this country has a great history. There are many historic monuments too. But visit the Crimea and you will see what is left of the once flourishing Crimean state! Visit the town of Stary Krym—the medieval city of Solkhat—where once there were 112 mosques with their pointed minarets, not to mention other buildings. Will you find there even one mosque, not for praying in (you must be joking!) but just as a monument of oriental architecture? Travel through all of the Crimea and will you find even one Muslim cemetery? I can assure you, your search would be in vain. . .

In the Crimea all our ancient monuments have been destroyed, with the exception of the palace of the Khans in Bakhchiserai, whose appearance has been changed during restoration and where tourists and holiday-makers visiting the museum are subjected to official propaganda directed against the Crimean Tatars.

You affirm that in the USSR you prayed in three different mosques and nobody hindered you. And on the basis of this you conclude that religion is flourishing in our country, 'you can pray as much as you like' you write. Praise Allah, today they do not thrust into our hands certificates that we are Godless, for the refusal of which people were imprisoned in the 1930s, and they do not demolish mosques. Today we have the right to attend places of worship. But you did not ask the question how many places of worship we have left and whether we have the opportunity to study God's word. You yourself affirm that in the USSR 'it is only not allowed to distribute literature of a religious nature on the streets or to preach or to convert people forcibly to one's faith. . .' But if we have the right to pray we ought to have the right to religious education. Korans, Bibles and other religious books are not sold in shops in the USSR, there are no religious schools. One might well ask, how am I supposed to benefit from my right to attend the mosque? Should I just go to look at the four walls, the floor and the ceiling? At the present time our young people are completely illiterate in religious matters. We are placed in circumstances in which our national and religious customs have disappeared irrevocably. We Crimean Tatars are deprived of the right not only to religious education but also to education in our own language, without which a people cannot survive as a nation and are therefore threatened with complete liquidation. . .

Reshat Dzhemilev   10 February 1979

(c) BUDDHISTS

As readers of Walter Kolarz's excellent chapter on the Buddhists in *Religion in the Soviet Union* will know, few religious denominations were as highly organized when the new regime took over in the Soviet Union. Only a brutal use of force could destroy the existing structure which bound together half a million people into an integrated unit. The spiritual leader of the community, Avgan Dordzhiev, a man of outstanding calibre, believed, furthermore, that Buddhist teachings were compatible with the building of a 'socialist society' on the Leninist model.

Stalin, always as severe to his near-sympathizers as to his outright opponents, crushed the whole structure of Soviet Buddhism with a severity which was experienced by few other religious groups in the USSR. There were about 120 Buddhist monasteries in the USSR in the early 1930s, but they had all been destroyed or closed down by 1938. The monastery at Ivolginsk, 25 miles south of Ulan-Ude in Buryatia, was however reopened after the Second World War.

This savage policy towards Buddhism has encouraged some commentators to go beyond the evidence, however. Nicholas Poppe wrote (*Religion in the USSR*, Munich 1960, p. 179) that the death of Dordzhiev in prison in 1938 'was the end of organized Buddhism in the USSR, of which not a single memorial remains. Nothing remains of the Buddhist temples in Buryatia and Kalmykia. The fate of Lamaism in the USSR deserves attention as an example of the complete destruction of a religious group as a whole.'

Not even the combined might of the Soviet secret police, atheist agencies and political commissars could in fact achieve such a result. The evidence of a revival in Soviet Buddhism has been mounting in recent years. Very importantly, a Buddhist Central Council was re-established after the Second World War, based at Ivolginsk, 25 miles south of Ulan-ude in Buryatia. This has not had the right of calling representatives assemblies, except for the purpose of electing first Lama Sharapov and then later Lama Gomboev as head of the Soviet Buddhists (Bandido Hambo Lama). The former election, in 1956, may have been rigged, for Lama Darmaev, the former holder of the office, had retired and his deputy had gone at the same time. Lama Sharapov at once became a most successful mouthpiece for the Soviet cause when required, especially in dealing with the Buddhist peoples of Asia.

There has been much more to the revival of Buddhism than the setting up of a propagandist Central Council. There may be now as many as 300 active Lamas on Soviet territory (excluding the Mongolian People's Republic, which falls outside the framework of the present study) though Soviet sources usually say there are no more than 'a few dozen'. What is certain, however, is that 'pilgrims constantly come to the datsan (monastary) at Ivolginsk, arriving on horseback, in cars and by aeroplane' (*Science and Religion*, Moscow, no. 7, 1961, p. 7). *The Propagandist's and Atheist's Handbook* (Moscow, 1966, p. 150) even admits that 'active religious propaganda in post-war years has succeeded in attracting a considerable number of young people into the religious communities'. Whether or not the claim of the Bandido Hambo Lama that 'practically every village in Buryatia still has its own lama' (*The Times*, 6 October 1970) is true, these small pieces of Soviet testimony demonstrate that the question of religious freedom for the Soviet Buddhist is still an important one.

A Soviet book on the subject, *Buddhism*, by A. N. Kochetov (Moscow, 1968), which has very few pages on the present internal situation, strongly suggests that normal religious practices undertaken by the lamas are treated as illegal. This implies that village communities are not able to exercise their legal rights and become registered:

'Lamas and those acting as such are infringing the legislation on religious cults; they carry out religious rites even in believers' houses and some practise traditional medicine. The lamas are resurrecting old customs, such as giving minors in marriage, collecting bride-money, etc.' (p. 156).

There has in recent years been a slanderous campaign against Buddhists in the Soviet press, though much of this has been in the local-language Buryat and Kalmyk newspapers which are not available in the West. But there have also been Russian-language articles, such as V. S. Ovchinnikov's 'The Reactionary and anti-Soviet activities of the Buryat Lamaist priesthood' (published in the Transbaikal Region Yearbook, 1967). Towards the end of 1972, news began to reach the West of new reprisals against Soviet Buddhists and Buddhist scholars. The outstanding name was that of Bidya Dandaron, a world-renowned Buddhist scholar and expert on the Tibetan language. Dandaron was arrested in late August and tried in December; he was sentenced to five years imprisonment with confiscation of property, on charges of founding a Buddhist sect. Documents on the case have demonstrated that the charge arose from the misunderstanding of a Tibetan word used by the group that had formed around Dandaron and which resembled the leader's name. In fact the group was an informal one consisting of Dandaron's pupils who met to learn about Buddhist philosophy and meditation. In September four members of the group were arrested and put in mental hospital. A further eight were to be tried but this case was subsequently dropped. A private letter to the West from a Soviet scholar and close friend of Dandaron, Alexander Pyatigorsky (now living in the West), stated: 'The objective evidently is to liquidate all study of Buddhism. . . This trial is patently the first act leading to much worse deeds. Times are worse than they have ever been since 1953'. These words rapidly proved to be only too true. In November 1974, news reached the West that Dandaron had died in his prison camp on 26 October 1974. He was 60. The exact circumstances of his death are not known, and may never be fully ascertained. His friends believe that he was singled out for especially harsh treatment by the authorities. It seems likely that he was ordered to return to work before serious injuries which he sustained in the autumn of 1973 were fully healed. He refused and was subsequently put in the punishment block. Dandaron's body was buried at the camp.

The main burden of the literature on contemporary Soviet Buddhism which is available to us concerns the enforced rooting out of old customs and their replacement by Soviet ones. Such campaigns are known to have had very limited success elsewhere and it seems most unlikely that the basic hostility of these Asian people to their European colonizers will have permitted them to embrace the ineptly-named 'new traditions' with anything approaching enthusiasm. One atheist article will talk of 'coloured ribbons fluttering in the breeze above the roofs of houses, adorned with texts of prayers and incantations against evil spirits' as a common feature in the villages of Buryatia (*Science and Religion*, no 7, 1961, p. 32). Another will describe the success of the secular replacements for just such old customs. There is contradiction and confusion among Soviet atheists—but Buddhism persists. Recent testimony to this fact has been borne by a Soviet newspaper *Uchitelskaya Gazeta* (Teacher's Gazette) which on 12 December 1972 spoke of the liveliness of Buddhism in Buryatia. The writer noted, for example, that 'When it was decided to send to the Mongolian Buddhist School for Monks a party of ten youths who had had secondary education, numbers of volunteers promptly appeared'. This article undoubtedly reflected the same official concern which resulted in the trial of Dandaron referred to above.

DOCUMENT 23:
TRANSCRIPT OF THE TRIAL OF THE BUDDHIST SCHOLAR B. D. DANDARON, ULAN-UDE, DECEMBER 1972

Translated from Arkhiv Samizdata *no. 1240. Slightly abbreviated.*

From 18 to 25 December there took place in Ulan-Ude, capital of the Buryat Republic, in the people's court of Oktyabrsky district, the trial of B. D. Dandaron. Born in 1914, he was a collaborator of the Buryat Institute of Social Sciences in the Siberian Section of the USSR Academy of Sciences (BISS), and one of the most outstanding Buddhist specialists.

The court consisted of the following officers:

I. Kh. Demin—president of the court

D. S. Dymbrylova—people's assessor

A. D. Merkel—ditto

A. F. Baiborodin—prosecutor

N. Ya. Nimirinskaya—defence counsel.

B. D. Dandaron, an outstanding Buddhist scholar and victim of the Stalinist repressions (he was sentenced in 1937 and served 19 years 8 months; rehabilitated in 1956) was sentenced to 5 years imprisonment with confiscation of property, to be served in an ordinary regime corrective labour colony (prosecutor Baiborodin asked for 8 years in a strict regime colony).

According to the Buryat procuracy's original plan, the trial was to have taken place as a grand condemnation of Buddhist believers. Besides Dandaron, who was charged with organizing and leading a Buddhist sect in 1971–2, eight more of his 'disciples' were supposed to appear before the court. The investigation charged them with active participation in a secret Buddhist sect, and with celebrating religious *sogshod* rituals at home, accompanied by 'bloody sacrifices'. These *sogshods* were supposed to have taken place in the flats of sect participants in Leningrad, Tartu, Ulan-Ude, Kizhinga. More than eighty witnesses were to have appeared, whose testimony was to have confirmed the existence of a 'sect' characterized by blind obedience to its 'teacher', his deification, a cult of violence expressed in a declaration of the 'necessity to destroy everything which hinders the Buddhist faith', sexual mysticism 'as a special norm of the Tantrist vow', ritual copulations, murder attempts and beating of 'former' members of the sect who wished to break with it, anti-Soviet attitudes and links with countries abroad and international Zionism.

Having intended to stage a grandiose trial of secret members of a Buddhist sect, the Buryat procuracy decided not to limit itself to the Buryat Republic. An all-Union framework was needed. This is why specialists and museum employees in Leningrad, Vilnius, etc., were arrested in the Dandaron 'case'. To the same end there were two searches at the home of O. F. Volkova, one of the main specialists on Sanskrit and Buddhist philosophy. 'Objects of the Buddhist cult' were confiscated, including two copies of the Bible and some Tibetan xylographs. In Moscow, not only O. F. Volkova was subjected to coarse and illiterate interrogations but also the important specialist on Buddhist philosophy A. M. Pyatigorsky and the well-known Tibetan specialist Yu. M. Parfyanovich, and in Tartu a teacher at Tartu University, L. E. Myall. The charges were based on the findings of a 'scientific-atheist, art-specialist' commission of experts. The main expert here was K. M. Gerasimova, head of the Buddhist Studies section at BISS and the second was a collaborator at the same institute, Dandaron's immediate superior, A. D. Dugar-Nimayev, who is not by any means a Buddhist specialist. In the findings of the 'commission of experts', K. M. Gerasimova permitted some obvious errors, or rather some deliberate distortions of the truth, since she, a Buddhist specialist, is responsible for such crude distortions as: ' . . . Buddhism is violence, it contains fanatical sects', and also the fabrications about sexual mysticism. Besides this, in the findings Gerasimova indulged in a series of observations going beyond her brief, representing direct attacks on Dandaron and criminal accusations. Gerasimova, who is preparing shortly to defend a doctoral dissertation at one of the Moscow or Leningrad institutes, was not present in court. The second 'expert', who was unable to answer a single one of the specialist questions by the defence counsel, refused to testify, saying that he was not competent in Buddhist questions.

During the trial almost all the charges were in effect dropped because they could not be proven and because of the unimpressive findings of the commission of experts and also 'testimonies' that did not inspire any confidence. . .

Before the trial there was an attempt to put pressure on the chief lama of Buryatia, Bandido Khambo Lama, but he refused to endorse the charges and refuted the accusation that Dandaron had founded a sect, explaining that *sogshods*, which include the giving of gifts to a teacher, can be held by anyone and anywhere, in the presence of any who wish to come. He also explained that during a *sogshod*, worship is paid not to the teacher but to the holy text.

The pre-planned spectacle had fallen through. Because of the publicity that had been given to the searches and interrogations of Moscow scholars and the reaction even outside the country, the Buryat procuracy decided not to bring them all to trial. . . The four arrested in Ulan-Ude, Yu. K. Lavrov, A. I. Zheleznov, D. Butkus and V. M. Mantlevich, were given a psychiatric investigation and without any grounds declared insane; it was resolved that they should have enforced treatment in special-type psychiatric institutions. The remainder, declared innocent of criminal responsibility, were dismissed from their jobs. . .

After the trial the court also took a special resolution to send a letter to the Leningrad Party committee on the weakness of ideological work in the city, on the grounds that most of those who had been involved in the trial were graduates of Leningrad colleges.

Angered by the failure of the intended spectacle, the Buryat procuracy and those who had inspired the trial decided to take it out on Dandaron alone. Regardless of the fact that the majority of the charges had been dropped, and also that the defence counsel N. A. Nimirinskaya in her four-hour speech had disproved all the remaining points and demonstrated her client's innocence, the court passed the following sentence:

B. D. Dandaron, born 1914. Sentenced in 1937 and 1948. Rehabilitated in 1956. Accused of crimes envisaged under articles 227/ I and 147/III of the Penal Code of the Russian Republic. Proofs of guilt:

1 All the participants in the group used to gather for *sogshod* prayer meetings, as confirmed both by Dandaron and his disciples.

2 An underground fund was established; Dandaron appointed

first Badmayev, then Lavrov as treasurer. This was confirmed by Dandaron, Badmayev, Aronov, Pupyshev and others.

3 From the findings of the scientific-atheist commission of experts it is clear that Buddhism entails worship, respect and deification of the teacher, and giving of gifts to him. Dandaron does not dispute that he was a teacher, witnesses Petrova, Repka, Albedil and many others confirmed that they worshipped him as a spiritual teacher. This is confirmed by reproductions of photographs of Dandaron in the robes of a lama.

The court found Dandaron guilty of crimes envisaged under articles 227/I and 147/III of the Russian Penal Code and on the basis of article 147/III decided to sentence him to five years imprisonment in an ordinary regime corrective labour colony.

It should be noted that in the course of the investigation and during the trial there was a huge number of procedural violations, including falsification of documents. . . In general, only those written testimonies and oral evidence which suited the court were taken into consideration, all the rest were ignored.

Of particular significance were the attempts to prevent the appearance of the witness L. E. Myall, since it was obvious that his evidence would contradict the line taken by the investigator-prosecutor. Even before the trial every effort was made to ensure that he would not be there. Thus he did not receive notification of the date of the trial, and the officials at the procuracy justified themselves by saying that they could not find a teacher at Tartu University, they could not phone Tartu University, etc. As a result Myall's notification somehow got to Leningrad and was handed to someone else who had absolutely no connection with the case. When Myall nevertheless reached Ulan-Ude, representatives of the Ministry of Internal Affairs (MVD) tried to arrest him at the entrance to the court, so as to prevent him attending the trial. Myall was forced to make two protests to the court against the attempt by Major Khamayev and his assistants to arrest him. However, immediately after giving his testimony, Myall was arrested on leaving the court building and taken to the procuracy where they demanded that he give his evidence. Myall refused, saying that he had just done so in court. Then they demanded that he testify as a witness in his own case. During the trial it was also declared that Myall's affair was being made into a separate 'case'.

A number of other procedural violations are known. For a long time defence counsel Nimirinskaya was refused permission to see her client alone, a right guaranteed by law (art. 201). She was able to avail herself of this right only after several protests and a declaration that she would protest to the Prosecutor-General Rudenko.

The most ominous figure in the trial was the prosecutor Baiborodin; he was also the chief investigator in the whole affair. The defence asked that the prosecutor be changed, but the court rejected her appeal. During the trial Baiborodin indulged in various insulting remarks: after the defence's protest and declaration that the prosecution had no right to speak of Dandaron as a criminal with two previous sentences, since her client was a victim of the Stalinist repressions and had been fully rehabilitated in 1956, Baiborodin declared: 'In Khrushchev's time they were rehabilitating anybody'. Also, as proof of the incompetence and abnormality of those involved in the trial, he stated that this was obvious from the fact that 'all intelligent people get out of Buryatia', and these had remained. It was because of such pearls of wisdom from the prosecutor that the defence requested a special resolution.

The final straw was the complete and open violation of the secrecy of the conference room: during the court's deliberations, MVD colonel Akhmedzyanov went in and stayed throughout the deliberations. The telephone was also ringing in the room the whole time.

An outstanding scholar and fine man has been sentenced to five years, having spent the best years of his life (from 23 to 43) in the most terrible Stalinist gaols. Many are amazed and are trying so understand the reasons for this 'Beilis trial' which seems so improbable in our time. But there is nothing improbable in this obscurantism—it is only one of a series of many trials against believers which are so characteristic of our happy times.